PRACTICE MAKES PERFECT

English Verbs

Loretta Gray

Mc Graw Hill

New York Chicago San Francisco Lisbon London Madrid Mexico City
Milan New Delhi San Juan Seoul Singapore Sydney Toronto

9 10 11 12 13 14 15 16 17 18 19 20 21 22 23 24 25 26   QPD/QPD   10

ISBN-13: 978-0-07-142646-6
ISBN-10:   0-07-142646-9
Library of Congress Control Number: 2004055924

McGraw-Hill books are available at special quantity discounts to use as premiums and sales promotions, or for use in corporate training programs. For more information, please write to the Director of Special Sales, Professional Publishing, McGraw-Hill, Two Penn Plaza, New York, NY 10121-2298. Or contact your local bookstore.

This book is printed on acid-free paper.

Contents

Contents

Introduction

When you study English verbs, you must do more than search for their meanings in a dictionary. You must also learn how to conjugate them and use these conjugations appropriately. Most students begin their studies by memorizing verb forms. They learn both the verb endings for regular verbs and the more complicated forms of the irregular verbs. *Practice Makes Perfect: English Verbs* provides you with opportunities to practice conjugating more than three hundred verbs, both regular and irregular.

However, this text is more than a list of verb forms and mechanical exercises. It also presents the reasons for choosing one verb form over another. For example, you may know the dictionary meaning of *walk*, but to use this verb to refer to the future, you must understand your options; that is, you must understand the role of tense and aspect. To indicate future, you could say *I'll walk to school today*, *I'm going to walk to school today*, or *I'm walking to school today*, but not *I walk to school today*.

When most people think of *tense*, they think of time. While it is true that tense is sometimes related to present, past, and future time, this is not always the case. In the sentence *My plane leaves in twenty minutes*, the simple present tense of the verb *leave* is used to refer to future time. As well as being marked for tense, verbs are marked for aspect. Aspect provides information about whether an action, a state, or an event has been completed and how a verb is related to other verbs in a time sequence. *I study English* and *I am studying English* are both in the present tense, but they differ in aspect. The verb in the first sentence refers to a habitual action; the verb in the second sentence refers to an action that is not yet completed. To indicate both tense and aspect, *study* is said to be in the simple present and *am studying* is said to be in the present progressive. In the sentence *I had been studying for the test when the phone rang*, there are two main verbs: *study* and *ring*. They are both in the past tense; however, they differ in aspect. *Had been studying* is the past perfect progressive, whereas *rang* is just the simple past. The difference in aspect indicates that the action of studying was ongoing and prior to the action of ringing. Tense and aspect intersect in the following way.

Tense/Aspect	present	past	future
simple	simple present	simple past	simple future
progressive	present progressive	past progressive	future progressive
perfect	present perfect	past perfect	future perfect
perfect progressive	present perfect progressive	past perfect progressive	future perfect progressive

The form and meaning of each of these tense-aspect combinations will be described in the units of this book. Although you will study all the tenses mentioned in traditional textbooks, you will also study the concept of aspect so that you will have a deeper understanding of the grammatical meaning conveyed by the form of a verb. Thus, as you work through the material in *Practice Makes Perfect: English Verbs*, you will learn not only how to conjugate verbs but also why to use specific verb forms.

Any study of verbs would be incomplete without the inclusion of special types of verbs and complementation patterns. After you become familiar with verb conjugations, you will study phrasal verbs, modal verbs, and verb complementation (gerunds and infinitives).

This book focuses on the verbs most frequently used in English. It is appropriate for classroom use or individual study. If you are in a class, your teacher may choose to assign exercises to supplement your other coursework. If you are studying alone, you can use the Answer Key at the back of the book to check your work and decide whether you should review a chapter or go on to the next.

There are six principal parts in this book:

PART I—THE PRESENT TENSE   The five units in Part I will help you learn the verb forms that constitute four different tense-aspect combinations: simple present, present progressive, present perfect, and present perfect progressive. You will practice using these forms in positive statements, negative statements, and questions. You will also learn how to form contractions with pronouns or the word *not*. A special section focuses on the verb *be*.

PART II—THE PAST TENSE   The five units in Part II will help you learn four more tense-aspect combinations: simple past, past progressive, past perfect, and past perfect progressive. As in Part I, you will practice using these tense-aspect combinations and their contracted forms in positive statements, negative statements, and questions. In this part also, there is a special section focusing on the verb *be*.

PART III—THE FUTURE TENSE   Part III differs from the others in that the modal *will* is introduced rather than verb endings. This part consists of five units: simple future, future progressive, future perfect, future perfect progressive, and a unit on the use of *be going to*. You will practice using the future tense-aspect combinations and their contracted forms in positive statements, negative statements, and questions.

PART IV—IMPERATIVE, PASSIVE, AND HYPOTHETICAL CONDITIONAL   The three units in Part IV will help you learn to use verbs in special constructions not discussed earlier: imperative (*Be careful!*), passive (*The project was finished on time.*), and hypothetical conditional (*If I were you, I would accept the offer.*).

PART V—PHRASAL VERBS AND MODAL AUXILIARY VERBS   The English language is full of phrasal verbs, which are verb-particle combinations, such as *run into* in *run into an old friend*. In the first unit of Part V, you will practice using some common phrasal verbs. The second unit of Part V focuses on modal auxiliary verbs. Although you will be introduced to modal verbs in Parts III and IV, you will learn more about the subtle shades of meaning that tense and aspect add to these verbs.

PART VI—GERUND AND INFINITIVE COMPLEMENTS   Some verbs take gerunds, some take infinitive complements, and some take both. Part VI will help you learn to choose appropriate verb complements.

Practice Makes Perfect: English Verbs ends with an appendix of irregular verb forms, followed by a glossary of grammatical terms.

PART I

THE PRESENT TENSE

Verbs in the present tense occur in four forms, each signaling a different aspect. (*Aspect* is explained in the Introduction.) Each of these forms conveys information about an action, state, or event that is relevant now.

SIMPLE PRESENT: I **study** every day.

PRESENT PROGRESSIVE: I **am studying** right now.

PRESENT PERFECT: I **have studied** English for two years.

PRESENT PERFECT PROGRESSIVE: I **have been studying** all day for my test tomorrow.

In the following units, you will learn about these verb forms and the reasons for using them.

Simple Present

When you refer to habitual actions, customs, and facts, use simple present verb forms.

> HABITUAL ACTION: I **work** in the library.

> CUSTOM: Most Americans **eat** turkey on Thanksgiving Day.

> FACT: The earth **revolves** around the sun.

If you include a time reference, you can also use the simple present to indicate future time.

> FUTURE ACTION: The concert **starts** in five minutes.

Except for *be* and *have*, verbs in the simple present follow this pattern:

	Singular	**Plural**
First Person	I **verb**	we **verb**
Second Person	you **verb**	you **verb**
Third Person	he, she, it **verb + s/es**	they **verb**

As you can see, the base form of the verb is used with the subject pronouns *I*, *you*, *we*, and *they* and with the nouns these pronouns can replace. For example, *the students* takes the same verb form as *they*. An ending, either *-s* or *-es*, is added to the verb when the subject pronoun is *he*, *she*, or *it* or a noun these pronouns can replace. The *-s* ending is used most frequently. The *-es* ending is used after certain letters or letter combinations.

Letters	Examples
s	pass + es
sh	push + es
ch	march + es
x	box + es
o	do + es
When a verb ends in a consonant and *y*, change the *y* to *i* and add *-es*.	bury → buries

The verb *be* is described in Unit 2. In the following chart are the forms of the verb *have*:

	Singular	Plural
First Person	I **have**	we **have**
Second Person	you **have**	you **have**
Third Person	he, she, it **has**	they **have**

Notice that *has* is the verb form used with *he, she, it,* and the nouns these pronouns can replace.

exercise   1-1

Complete each sentence with the simple present form of the verb in parentheses. Circle the reason that the simple present is used.

1. I _____ (eat) lunch in the cafeteria every day but Friday.

   Habitual action   **Custom**   **Fact**   **Future time**

2. Julia _____ (carry) a heavy backpack to school every day.

   Habitual action   **Custom**   **Fact**   **Future time**

3. You _____ (speak) English well.

   Habitual action   **Custom**   **Fact**   **Future time**

4. The state of Florida _____ (produce) a great deal of citrus fruit.

   Habitual action   **Custom**   **Fact**   **Future time**

5. During the holidays, we always _____ (make) special meals.

   Habitual action   **Custom**   **Fact**   **Future time**

6. He _____ (watch) television every night.

   Habitual action   **Custom**   **Fact**   **Future time**

7. My roommate _____ (say) a prayer before he eats.

   Habitual action   **Custom**   **Fact**   **Future time**

8. The game _____ (begin) in an hour.

   Habitual action   **Custom**   **Fact**   **Future time**

9. My friends and I _____ (live) near a park.

   Habitual action   **Custom**   **Fact**   **Future time**

10. Trees _____ (grow) tall in the Pacific Northwest.

    Habitual action   **Custom**   **Fact**   **Future time**

11. We _____ (wear) traditional dress on holidays.

    Habitual action   **Custom**   **Fact**   **Future time**

12. Most people _____ (shake) hands when they first _____ (meet).

    Habitual action   **Custom**   **Fact**   **Future time**

exercise	1-2

Using the pronoun and verb provided, create your own sentences.

1. She always (make) _____.

2. I (take) _____.

3. It (give) _____.

4. They (come) _____.

5. I (use) _____.

6. He (leave) _____.

7. They (like) _____.

8. She (write) _____.

9. We (listen) _____.

10. It (contain) _____.

11. It (start) _____.

12. He (understand) _____.

Forming Negatives

To make a verb negative, add the auxiliary verb *do* and the word *not* before the main verb.

    do not go   does not like

Remember that *does* is used with the pronouns *he, she,* and *it*. When *does* is used, the main verb has no *-s* or *-es* ending.

exercise   1-3

Make each of the following sentences negative.

EXAMPLE: I spend a lot of money.
I do not spend a lot of money.

1. He goes to school every day.

   _____

2. My roommate likes snakes.

   _____

3. You know my family.

   _____

4. The owner opens the store every day at 8:00.

   _____

5. We help our neighbors.

   _____

6. My friends send me letters.

   _____

7. I feel tired.

   _____

8. She speaks five different languages.

   _____

9. They study in the library.

   _____

10. We listen to pop music.

    _____

11. They grow tomatoes in their backyard.

    _____

12. This car runs well.

    _____

Forming Contractions

In English, verbs are often combined with other words to form contractions. These shortened forms include an apostrophe (') to indicate missing letters. It is important to learn contractions because you will often hear them in conversation or see them in informal writing. Formal writing, though, rarely contains contractions.

The auxiliary verb *do* is often combined with *not* to form a contraction. Notice that an apostrophe indicates that the letter *o* is omitted:

do + not = don't   does + not = doesn't

 **1-4**

Rewrite the sentences in exercise 1-3 using contractions.

1. _____

2. _____

3. _____

4. _____

5. _____

6. _____

7. _____

8. _____

9. _____

10. _____

11. _____

12. _____

Forming Yes/No Questions

To form questions that can be answered yes or no (yes/no questions), begin the question with the auxiliary verb *do*. After the auxiliary verb, place the subject and the main verb.

Statement: He rides his bicycle to school.
Yes/no question: Does he ride his bicycle to school?

Statement: They ride the bus to work.
Yes/no question: Do they ride the bus to work?

exercise	1-5

Rewrite the following statements as yes/no questions.

> EXAMPLE: You get tired easily.
> *Do you get tired easily?*

1. The artist shows his work at a local gallery.

   _____

2. They meet on Thursday mornings.

   _____

3. She works hard.

   _____

4. You commute to work.

   _____

5. It seems like a good decision.

   _____

6. This work requires patience.

   _____

7. The Carsons live in a small town.

   _____

8. You don't believe my story. (Notice that *do* has already been used to indicate negation.)

   _____

9. The patient feels better.

   _____

10. The lecture ends at 5:30.

    _____

11. The plot involves many characters.

    _____

12. Most students complete the program in four years.

    _____

Forming *Wh*-Questions

Wh-questions are used to elicit specific pieces of information. They usually begin with *what, who, why, where, when, how,* or combinations such as *how much, how many,* and *how often.* When the question word is the subject of the sentence, the form of the question is similar to the form of a statement.

       Statement: Max needs a new key.
       Wh-question: Who needs a new key?

       Statement: Something is wrong.
       Wh-question: What is wrong?

When the question word is any other part of the sentence, the auxiliary verb *do* comes after the question word and is followed by the subject and the main verb.

       Statement: She collects butterflies.
       Wh-question: What does she collect?

       Statement: They live on the coast of Maine.
       Wh-question: Where do they live?

 **exercise   1-6**

Complete the following questions based on the statements provided.

    EXAMPLE: The performance starts at 7:00.
              When *does the performance start?*

1. The person in the back row knows the answer.

   Who _____

2. She looks healthy.

   How _____

3. They always go to that restaurant because they like the food.

   Why _____

4. They go golfing twice a week.

   How often _____

5. We turn left at the corner.

   Where _____

6. The notebook costs $3.00.

   How much _____

7. My mother worries too much.

   Who _____

8. You exercise every day at the gym.

   How often _____

9. Jerry and Carol repair computers.

   What _____

10. She teaches English.

    What _____

11. Mark blames other people for his problems.

    Whom _____
    (*Who* may be used instead of *whom* in conversation and informal writing.)

12. Many people go to Cape Cod for their vacations.

    Where _____

Be Verb Forms

The verb *be* has three different forms in the simple present: *am, is,* and *are.*

	Singular	Plural
First Person	I **am**	we **are**
Second Person	you **are**	you **are**
Third Person	he, she, it **is**	they **are**

exercise   **2-1**

Complete each sentence with the simple present form of the verb be.

1. I _____ a student.

2. You _____ taller than I _____.

3. My parents _____ on vacation.

4. Misuzu _____ from San Francisco.

5. My roommate's name _____ Chris.

6. They _____ late again.

7. We _____ ready for the test.

8. I _____ interested in all kinds of sports.

9. It _____ easy.

10. Your coat _____ in the closet.

11. She _____ the director.

12. They _____ in class together.

The word *there* is often used with the verb *be* to acknowledge the existence of someone or something. The form of the *be* verb is based on the subject that follows it.

SINGULAR SUBJECT: There **is a concert** in the park tonight.
PLURAL SUBJECT: There **are four rooms** in the house.

exercise   2-2

Circle the verb that agrees in number with the subject that follows it.

1. There **is**/**are** someone at the door.

2. There **is**/**are** several parks in the town.

3. There **is**/**are** fifty-two cards in a deck.

4. There **is**/**are** a restroom at the end of the hall.

5. There **is**/**are** sixteen students in the class.

6. There **is**/**are** a bank on the corner of Lincoln and Ash.

7. There **is**/**are** an information booth in the lobby.

8. There **is**/**are** many specialty stores in the Mall of America.

9. There **is**/**are** still tickets available.

10. There **is**/**are** a typo on page 3.

11. There **is**/**are** a huge fountain in front of the building.

12. There **is**/**are** only one possible answer to the question.

Forming Contractions: Pronouns and *There* with *Am, Is,* and *Are*

Contractions are often formed by combining pronouns and the verb *be*. The word *there* can also be combined with *be*. It is important to learn these contractions because you will often hear them in conversation or see them in informal writing. However, you should avoid using them in formal writing.

Notice that an apostrophe indicates that a letter is omitted:

I + am = I'm   we + are = we're
you + are = you're   they + are = they're
he + is = he's   there + is = there's
she + is = she's   it + is = it's

exercise   **2-3**

Rewrite each sentence using a contraction.

EXAMPLE: He is not here today.
He's not here today.

1. She is a student.

_____

2. I am an engineer.

_____

3. There is a test on Tuesday.

_____

4. You are next.

_____

5. It is difficult.

_____

6. We are from Canada.

_____

7. He is a supervisor.

_____

8. They are really funny.

_____

9. I am sick today.

_____

10. There is a package for you on the table.

_____

11. He is first on the list.

_____

12. It is cold in here.

_____

Forming Negatives

To make the verb *be* negative, just add *not*.

am not	is not	are not
I'm not	it's not	we're not

 2-4

Using contractions, make each of the sentences in exercise 2-3 negative.

1. _____

2. _____

3. _____

4. _____

5. _____

6. _____

7. _____

8. _____

9. _____

10. _____

11. _____

12. _____

Forming Contractions: *Isn't* and *Aren't*

The word *not* can be contracted with the verb forms *is* and *are*.

is + not = isn't   are + not = aren't

 2-5

Complete the sentences using either isn't *or* aren't.

1. There _____ a ball game tonight.

2. There _____ any rooms available.

3. There _____ a full moon tonight.

4. There _____ any cookies left.

5. There _____ many people here today.

6. There _____ much time.

Forming Yes/No Questions

To form yes/no questions, begin the question with a form of the verb *be* and place the subject after it.

> Statement: Nancy is a doctor.
> Yes/no question: Is Nancy a doctor?

> Statement: They are friendly.
> Yes/no question: Are they friendly?

To form yes/no questions with *there*, place *there* after the *be* verb.

> Statement: There is a gas station near the freeway.
> Yes/no question: Is there a gas station near the freeway?

exercise 2-6

Rewrite the following statements as yes/no questions.

> EXAMPLE: It is late.
> *Is it late?*

1. Portland is in the state of Oregon.

   _____

2. Your car is in the garage.

   _____

3. He is in a good mood.

   _____

4. They are friends.

   _____

5. Sam is depressed.

   _____

6. Her computer is broken.

   _____

7. There are many items on the menu.

   _____

8. The coffee is too hot.

   _____

9. The city hall is the oldest building in town.

   _____

10. There is a bank near here.

    _____

11. The museum is open on Thursday evenings.

    _____

12. The lights are off.

    _____

Forming *Wh*-Questions

To form *wh*-questions, place the *be* verb after the question word. When the question word is the subject of the sentence, the form of the question is similar to the form of a statement.

> Statement: Someone is at the door.
> *Wh*-question: Who is at the door?

When the question word is any other part of the sentence, the subject follows the *be* verb.

> Statement: She is from Colorado.
> *Wh*-question: Where is she from?

> Statement: His birthday is July 11.
> *Wh*-question: When is his birthday?

exercise	2-7

Complete the following questions based on the statements provided.

> EXAMPLE: You are twenty-two years old.
>   How old *are you?*

1. Kevin Lee is the editor of the local newspaper.

   Who _____

2. She is five feet tall.

   How tall _____

3. They are visitors from another school.

   Who _____

4. His roommate is at work right now.

   Where _____

5. The graduation ceremony is on Saturday.

   When _____

6. The house is white.

   What color _____

7. That is a bike lock.

   What _____

8. The scissors are in the drawer.

   Where _____

9. Sandy Craig is the producer.

   Who _____

10. The children are at their grandmother's house.

    Where _____

11. The library is open until 8:00.

    How late _____

12. They are in the cafeteria.

    Where _____

Present Progressive (*Be* Verb + *-ing*)

When you refer to a temporary situation or an activity in progress, use the present progressive.

> TEMPORARY SITUATION: I **am working** in the library this term.

> ACTIVITY IN PROGRESS: She **is studying** right now.

If you include a time reference, you can also use the present progressive to indicate future time.

> FUTURE TIME: My parents **are coming** *tomorrow.*

The present progressive consists of the auxiliary verb *be* and the *-ing* form of the main verb. The auxiliary verb is marked for tense.

	Singular	Plural
First Person	I **am verb** + **ing**	we **are verb** + **ing**
Second Person	you **are verb** + **ing**	you **are verb** + **ing**
Third Person	he, she, it **is verb** + **ing**	they **are verb** + **ing**

When a one-syllable word or a word with a stressed final syllable ends in a single consonant sound, double the last letter before adding *-ing*.

> One-syllable word: run → running

> Word ending in a stressed syllable: admit → admitting

> BUT mow → mowing [This word ends in a vowel sound.]

When a word ends with a consonant and the letter *e*, drop the *e* before adding *-ing*: come → coming. The letter *e* is not dropped from words such as *be, see,* and *free.*

exercise   **3-1**

Complete each sentence with the present progressive form of the verb in parentheses. Circle the reason that the present progressive is used.

1. I _____ (study) English this term.

   Temporary situation   **Activity in progress**   **Future time**

2. We _____ (go) home tomorrow.

   Temporary situation   **Activity in progress**   **Future time**

3. Right now, I _____ (write) a letter.

   Temporary situation   **Activity in progress**   **Future time**

4. The bus _____ (pull) up to the curb at this very moment.

   Temporary situation   **Activity in progress**   **Future time**

5. They _____ (move) to Florida at the end of the month.

   Temporary situation   **Activity in progress**   **Future time**

6. The kids _____ (act) silly right now.

   Temporary situation   **Activity in progress**   **Future time**

7. I _____ (use) my friend's car today.

   Temporary situation   **Activity in progress**   **Future time**

8. We _____ (eat) early tonight.

   Temporary situation   **Activity in progress**   **Future time**

9. The company _____ (have) problems this year.

   Temporary situation   **Activity in progress**   **Future time**

10. My neighbor _____ (mow) his lawn.

    Temporary situation   **Activity in progress**   **Future time**

11. I _____ (turn) in my paper tomorrow.

    Temporary situation   **Activity in progress**   **Future time**

12. Steve _____ (live) with his cousin this year.

    Temporary situation   **Activity in progress**   **Future time**

13. It _____ (snow).

    Temporary situation   **Activity in progress**   **Future time**

14. Several police officers _____ (stand) in front of the store.

    Temporary situation   **Activity in progress**   **Future time**

15. You _____ (speak) too loudly.

    Temporary situation   **Activity in progress**   **Future time**

16. The sky _____ (grow) dark.

    Temporary situation   **Activity in progress**   **Future time**

exercise   3-2

Complete each sentence with either the simple present or the present progressive. If you need help, review pages 3–4 and 19.

1. Jim _____ (sell) cars for a living.

2. Jim _____ (sell) his car to his sister.

3. I _____ (boil) some water for tea.

4. Water _____ (boil) at one hundred degrees centigrade.

5. We always _____ (visit) our grandparents during the holidays.

6. This year we _____ (visit) our grandparents during the holidays.

7. Jean _____ (go) to a lot of movies.

8. Jean _____ (go) to a movie today.

9. I _____ (do) my homework right now.

10. I generally _____ (do) my homework in the evening.

Forming Contractions: Pronouns with the Auxiliary Verb *Be*

Contractions are often formed by combining a pronoun and the auxiliary verb *be*. You will often hear these contractions in conversation or see them in informal writing, but you will rarely find them used in formal contexts.

Notice that an apostrophe indicates that a letter is omitted:

I + am = I'm moving   we + are = we're moving
you + are = you're moving   they + are = they're moving
he + is = he's moving
she + is = she's moving
it + is = it's moving

exercise   3-3

Use the pronoun and verb given to create a sentence that contains a contraction.

EXAMPLE: I, follow
I'm following in my parents' footsteps.

1. He, pay

_____

2. It, hail

_____

3. We, meet

_____

4. They, lose

_____

5. She, wait

_____

6. You, carry

_____

7. I, wear

_____

8. We, read

_____

9. She, call

_____

10. He, sell

_____

11. They, stay

_____

12. I, assist

_____

Forming Negatives

To make a present progressive verb negative, place *not* after the auxiliary verb.

am not going   is not going   are not going

exercise	3-4

Make each of the following sentences negative.

EXAMPLE: We are ordering pizza for dinner tonight.
We are not ordering pizza for dinner tonight.

1. I am buying a new car tomorrow.

_____

2. She is studying.

_____

3. We are leaving soon.

_____

4. They are coming with us.

_____

5. Carla is living with her parents.

_____

6. I am cooking dinner tonight.

_____

7. The band is performing tonight.

_____

8. My mother is visiting this weekend.

_____

9. They are sleeping.

_____

10. We are going to the park today.

   _____

11. They are fixing the road.

   _____

12. She is quitting her job.

   _____

Forming Contractions: Pronouns with *Am Not, Is Not,* and *Are Not*

The following contractions can be used in conversation and informal writing:

I'm not going

He's not working
He isn't working
She's not working
She isn't working
It's not working
It isn't working

You're not working
You aren't working
We're not working
We aren't working
They're not working
They aren't working

exercise   3-5

Rewrite the sentences in exercise 3-4 using contractions.

1. _____

2. _____

3. _____

4. _____

5. _____

6. _____

7. _____

8. _____

9. _____

10. _____

11. _____

12. _____

Forming Yes/No Questions

To form yes/no questions, begin the question with the auxiliary verb *be*. After the auxiliary verb, place the subject and the *-ing* form of the main verb.

Statement: Prices are falling.
Yes/no question: Are prices falling?

Rewrite the following statements as yes/no questions.

EXAMPLE: You are finishing your paper.
Are you finishing your paper?

1. The mail carrier is delivering a package to our house.

   _____

2. The boat is sinking.

   _____

3. They are causing trouble.

   _____

4. He is worrying about his course grade.

   _____

5. Helen is publishing her autobiography.

   _____

6. The teacher is inviting everyone in class to a party.

   _____

7. The committee is announcing the winner of the contest today.

   _____

8. The engineer is explaining the process.

   _____

9. Mandy is singing at her sister's wedding.

   _____

10. The company is expanding.

    _____

11. Phil is arranging the conference.

   _____

12. The police are accusing him of the crime.

   _____

Forming *Wh*-Questions

In *wh*-questions, when the question word is the subject of the sentence, the form of the question is similar to the form of a statement.

>   Statement: Someone is talking on the telephone.
>   *Wh*-question: Who is talking on the telephone?

When the question word is any other part of the sentence, the auxiliary verb *be* comes after the question word and is followed by the subject and the *-ing* form of the main verb.

>   Statement: They are going to the store.
>   *Wh*-question: Where are they going?

>   Statement: He is writing a play.
>   *Wh*-question: What is he writing?

| exercise | 3-7 |

Complete the following questions based on the statements provided.

>   EXAMPLE: We are leaving in the morning.
>   When *are we leaving*?

1. They are eating pasta salad.

   What _____

2. Fran is coming along.

   Who _____

3. We are watching the soccer game on television tonight.

   What _____

4. She is showing them some of her new paintings.

   What _____

5. You are meeting the director.

   Whom _____
   (*Who* may be used instead of *whom* in conversation and informal writing.)

6. They are wearing special clothes because it is a holiday.

   Why _____

7. He is hoping for a new job.

   What _____

8. Something strange is happening.

   What _____

9. Alex and Terry are playing Scrabble.

   What _____

10. They are moving to Mexico.

    Where _____

11. Somebody is staring at us.

    Who _____

12. Venus Williams is winning.

    Who _____

Present Perfect

Use the present perfect when you want to refer to a situation that originated in the past but continues into the present or to refer to a past experience that has current relevance.

PAST SITUATION CONTINUING INTO THE PRESENT: I **have lived** in Dallas for six years.

PAST EXPERIENCE WITH CURRENT RELEVANCE: We **have traveled** to Alaska three times.

For an experience to be relevant, it is usually related to a possible future experience. In the example "We have traveled to Alaska three times," the speaker may be considering another trip. The present perfect is often used in job interviews when an employer asks a prospective employee about his or her experience: "Have you ever driven a large vehicle?" "Have you ever used a cash register?"

The present perfect consists of the auxiliary verb *have* and the perfect/passive form of the main verb. The auxiliary verb is marked for tense. The perfect/passive verb form is used to indicate either the perfect aspect or the passive voice. (The passive voice will be discussed in Part IV.) The perfect/passive form for regular verbs consists of the base form of the verb and the ending *-ed*.

	Singular	Plural
First Person	I **have verb + ed**	we **have verb + ed**
Second Person	you **have verb + ed**	you **have verb + ed**
Third Person	he, she, it **has verb + ed**	they **have verb + ed**

When a one-syllable word or a word with a stressed final syllable ends in a single consonant sound, double the last letter before adding *-ed*.

One-syllable word: pet → petted

Word ending in a stressed syllable: admit → admitted

BUT sew → sewed [This word ends in a vowel sound.]

The present/passive forms of irregular verbs can be found in the appendix.

The following are common irregular verb patterns:

- Pattern 1: The final *d* becomes a *t*.

buil**d**	buil**t**
len**d**	len**t**
spen**d**	spen**t**

- Pattern 2: A *-d* or *-t* suffix is added. The vowel changes.

feel /fil/	felt /fɛlt/
keep /kip/	kept /kɛpt/
sell /sɛl/	sold /sold/

- Pattern 3: An *-n* or *-en* suffix is added.

eat	eaten
fall	fallen
know	known

Sometimes the vowel changes.

speak /spik/	spoken /spokɛn/
wear /wɛr/	worn /worn/

- Pattern 4: Just the vowel changes.

hold /hold/	held /hɛld/
meet /mit/	met /mɛt/
sit /sɪt/	sat /sæt/

- Pattern 5: The base form and perfect/passive form are the same.

put	put
hit	hit
cut	cut

exercise   4-1

Complete each sentence with the present perfect form of the verb in parentheses. If you are unsure of the perfect/passive form, check the chart in the appendix.

1. Pat and Tom _____ (build) two houses this summer.

2. I _____ (eat) already.

3. His parents _____ (lend) him some money.

4. We _____ (speak) to the director about our concerns.

5. The company's stock _____ (fall).

6. You _____ (know) me for a long time.

7. They _____ (sell) their house.

8. It _____ (rain) every day for a week.

9. I _____ (keep) your secret.

10. He _____ (spend) too much money this month.

11. The bride and groom _____ (cut) the wedding cake.

Forming Contractions: Pronouns with the Auxiliary Verb *Have*

Contractions are often formed by combining a pronoun and the auxiliary verb *have*. You will often hear these contractions in conversation or see them in informal writing, but you will rarely find them used in formal contexts.

Notice that an apostrophe indicates the omission of the letters *h* and *a*:

I + have = I've moved
you + have = you've moved
he + has = he's moved
she + has = she's moved
it + is = it's moved

we + have = we've moved
they + have = they've moved

 **exercise   4-2**

Use the pronoun and verb given to create a sentence that contains a contraction.

EXAMPLE: I, ask
I've asked too many questions.

1. He, rent

   _____ an apartment for the summer.

2. It, work

   _____ until now.

3. We, be

   _____ friends for a long time.

4. They, lose

   _____ another game.

5. She, wait

   _____ a long time.

6. You, reach

   _____ your goal.

7. I, apply

    _____ for a new job.

8. We, develop

    _____ some new software.

9. She, ignore

    _____ our advice.

10 He, find

    _____ his keys.

11. They, go

    _____ home.

12. I, forget

    _____ my books.

Forming Negatives

To make a present perfect verb negative, place *not* after the auxiliary verb.

        has not gone   have not gone

 **4-3**

Make each of the following sentences negative.

        EXAMPLE: We have calculated the cost.
                 We have not calculated the cost.

1. They have chosen a location for the conference.

    _____

2. She has completed her work.

    _____

3. We have studied our options.

    _____

4. I have received my test results.

    _____

5. You have mentioned his name before.

    _____

6. He has reviewed the plans.

_____

7. It has disappeared.

_____

Forming Contractions: *Hasn't* and *Haven't*

The following contractions can be used in conversation and informal writing:

I haven't gone   We haven't gone
You haven't gone   They haven't gone
He hasn't gone
She hasn't gone
It hasn't gone

 **exercise   4-4**

Rewrite the sentences in exercise 4-3 using contractions.

1. _____

2. _____

3. _____

4. _____

5. _____

6. _____

7. _____

Forming Yes/No Questions

To form yes/no questions, begin the question with the auxiliary verb *have*. After the auxiliary verb, place the subject and the perfect/passive form of the main verb.

Statement: His personality has changed.
Yes/no question: Has his personality changed?

Rewrite the following statements as yes/no questions.

> EXAMPLE: She has followed the directions.
> *Has she followed the directions?*

1. You have put the dishes away.

   _____

2. They have offered her a new job.

   _____

3. We have received good news.

   _____

4. He has checked the oil in the car.

   _____

5. Jackson has obtained a driver's license.

   _____

6. The new student has arrived.

   _____

7. Jeanette has responded to our message.

   _____

8. The archaeologists have discovered new fossils.

   _____

9. You have made your lunch.

   _____

10. The business has expanded.

    _____

11. Sarah has arranged the meeting.

    _____

12. The program has been successful.

    _____

Forming *Wh*-Questions

In *wh*-questions, when the question word is the subject of the sentence, the form of the question is similar to the form of a statement.

> Statement: Michael has represented us.
> *Wh*-question: Who has represented us?

When the question word is any other part of the sentence, the auxiliary verb *have* comes after the question word and is followed by the subject and the perfect/passive form of the main verb.

> Statement: They have collected old cars.
> *Wh*-question: What have they collected?

> Statement: You have moved three times.
> *Wh*-question: How many times have you moved?

Complete the following questions based on the statements provided.

> EXAMPLE: Scott has prevented an accident.
> Who *has prevented an accident?*

1. They have given computers to charities.

   What _____

2. The governor has appeared on television.

   Who _____

3. She has missed three games.

   How many games _____

4. Dan has passed the first part of the test.

   Who _____

5. You have read three of his novels.

   How many of his novels _____

6. Les has painted his house green.

   What color _____

7. She has sung at the White House.

   Who _____

8. Something unbelievable has happened.

   What _____

9. She has influenced your decision.

   Who _____

10. He has taken all of the required courses.

    Which courses _____

11. You have taught English for fifteen years.

    How many years _____

12. They have invited everyone in class to the party.

    Whom _____
    (*Who* may be used instead of *whom* in conversation and informal writing.)

Present Perfect Progressive

When you want to refer to an action, a state, or an event that originated in the past but is still ongoing or incomplete, use the present perfect progressive.

> ONGOING STATE: **I have been living** on a ship for three months.

> INCOMPLETE ACTION: **We have been organizing** this trip since May.

The present perfect progressive consists of two auxiliary verbs, *have* and *be*, and the *-ing* form of the main verb. The auxiliary verb *have* comes first, and it is marked for tense. Next comes the perfect/passive form of the verb *be—been*. The final element of the present perfect progressive is the *-ing* form of the main verb.

	Singular	**Plural**
First Person	I **have been verb + ing**	we **have been verb + ing**
Second Person	you **have been verb + ing**	you **have been verb + ing**
Third Person	he, she, it **has been verb + ing**	they **have been verb + ing**

exercise   5-1

Complete each sentence with the present perfect progressive form of the verb in parentheses.

1. My knee _____ (hurt) for a week.

2. The new policy _____ (cause) some confusion.

3. Janice _____ (exercise) for an hour.

4. I _____ (drink) a lot of coffee today.

5. He _____ (worry) too much.

6. She _____ (earn) good grades in all her classes.

7. Her parents _____ (pay) for her apartment.

8. We _____ (follow) your instructions.

9. We _____ (sit) here too long.

10. I _____ (apply) for scholarships.

11. They _____ (help) each other.

12. Temperatures _____ (rise).

Forming Contractions: Pronouns with the Auxiliary Verb *Have*

Contractions can be formed by combining a pronoun and the auxiliary verb *have*. You will often hear these contractions in conversation or see them in informal writing, but you will rarely find them used in formal contexts.

Notice that an apostrophe indicates the omission of the letters *h* and *a*:

I + have = I've been living   we + have = we've been living
you + have = you've been living   they + have = they've been living
he + has = he's been living
she + has = she's been living
it + has = it's been living

exercise   5-2

Use the pronoun and verb given to create a sentence that contains a contraction.

Example: We, hope
We've been hoping for better weather.

1. He, expect

_____ a phone call.

2. It, change

_____ day by day.

3. We, develop

_____ a new game.

4. They, check

_____ their e-mail every day.

5. She, explore

_____ her new home.

6. You, complain

_____ about your sore back all day.

7. I, calculate

_____ my income tax.

Forming Negatives

To make a present perfect progressive verb negative, place *not* after the auxiliary verb *have*.

has not been going   have not been going

Complete each of the following sentences using the subject and verb provided.

EXAMPLE: We, fall, not
We have not been falling behind in our work.

1. He, ignore, not

_____ the evidence.

2. It, improve, not

_____ much.

3. We, commute, not

_____ together this year.

4. They, buy, not

_____ much lately.

5. She, do, not

_____ her work.

6. You, finish, not

_____ your projects on time.

7. I, ride, not

_____ the bus to school.

Forming Contractions: *Hasn't* and *Haven't*

The following contractions can be used in conversation and informal writing:

I haven't been going   We haven't been going
You haven't been going   They haven't been going
He hasn't been going
She hasn't been going
It hasn't been going

exercise   5-4

Rewrite the sentences in exercise 5-3 using contractions.

1. _____

2. _____

3. _____

4. _____

5. _____

6. _____

7. _____

Forming Yes/No Questions

To form yes/no questions, begin the question with the auxiliary verb *have*. After a tensed form of *have*, place the subject, the perfect/passive form of the auxiliary verb *be* (*been*), and the *-ing* form of the main verb.

Statement: You have been tiring easily.
Yes/no question: Have you been tiring easily?

exercise   5-5

Rewrite the following statements as yes/no questions.

EXAMPLE: She has been using the new database.
Has she been using the new database?

1. You have been paying all your bills on time.

_____

2. The noise has been bothering them.

_____

3. Traffic has been moving slowly.

   _____

4. She has been waiting a long time.

   _____

5. They have been reducing the number of accidents.

   _____

6. The suspect has been lying.

   _____

7. You have been reading an interesting novel.

   _____

8. The government has been allowing journalists into the country.

   _____

9. She has been keeping good records.

   _____

10. They have been considering the proposal.

    _____

11. He has been staying close to home.

    _____

12. She has been making progress.

    _____

Forming Wh-Questions

In *wh*-questions, when the question word is the subject of the sentence, the form of the question is similar to the form of a statement.

> Statement: Brad Omans has been reporting the news.
> *Wh*-question: Who has been reporting the news?

When the question word is any other part of the sentence, the auxiliary verb *have* comes after the question word and is followed by the subject, the perfect/passive form of the auxiliary verb *be* (*been*), and the *-ing* form of the main verb.

> Statement: Many people have been going to the carnival.
> *Wh*-question: Where have many people been going?

> Statement: You have been looking at something.
> *Wh*-question: What have you been looking at?

exercise   5-6

Complete the following questions based on the statements provided.

      EXAMPLE: Barbara has been studying at night.
                When *has Barbara been studying?*

1. Paula has been traveling all over Asia.

   Where _____

2. He has been living in Miami for five years.

   How long _____

3. They have been searching for their lost dog.

   What _____

4. My grandfather has been watching the children.

   Who _____

5. They have been going to the Virgin Islands every spring.

   How often _____

6. The guide has been arranging a special tour of the ruins.

   What _____

7. Pei-Hsuan has been taking notes.

   Who _____

8. You have been attending the university since 2002.

   How long _____

9. They have been planning a surprise party for Marta.

   What _____

10. He has been talking about his new design.

    What _____

11. You have been feeling better lately.

    How _____

12. She has been standing there for two hours.

    How long _____

Summary of Tense-Aspect Combinations

TENSE/ASPECT	PRESENT
simple	simple present: *talk, talks*
progressive	present progressive: *am/is/are talking*
perfect	present perfect: *has/have talked*
perfect progressive	present perfect progressive: *has/have been talking*

PART II

THE PAST TENSE

Verbs in the past tense occur in four forms, each signaling a different aspect. (*Aspect* is explained in the Introduction.) These forms convey information about actions, states, or events that are remote in the speaker's mind. The past tense most often refers to past time.

SIMPLE PAST: I **waited** patiently.

PAST PROGRESSIVE: I **was waiting** for a bus.

PAST PERFECT: I **had waited** long enough.

PAST PERFECT PROGRESSIVE: I **had been waiting** for three hours.

In the following units, you will learn about these verb forms and the reasons for using them.

Simple Past

When you refer to past or completed actions, states, or events, use simple past verb forms.

> COMPLETED ACTION: We **drove** three hundred miles.

> PAST STATE: They **seemed** uneasy.

> PAST EVENT: The schedule **changed**.

You can also use the simple past to refer to a hypothetical action, state, or event.

> HYPOTHETICAL ACTION: If you **joined** our team, we could win the championship.

Sentences such as this one will be discussed in more detail in Part IV.

The simple past for regular verbs consists of the verb and the ending *-ed*.

	Singular	Plural
First Person	I **verb + ed**	we **verb + ed**
Second Person	you **verb + ed**	you **verb + ed**
Third Person	he, she, it **verb + ed**	they **verb + ed**

For regular verbs, the simple past form and the perfect/passive form (see pages 29–30) are the same.

When a one-syllable word or a word with a stressed final syllable ends in a single consonant sound, double the last letter before adding *-ed.*

> One-syllable word: plan → planned

> Word ending in a stressed syllable: occur → occurred

> BUT row → rowed [This word ends in a vowel sound.]

Irregular verbs have a variety of simple past forms, which can be found in the appendix.

The following are common irregular verb patterns. Some of these irregular simple past forms are the same as the perfect/passive forms.

- Pattern 1: The final *d* becomes a *t.* (Same as perfect/passive)

sen**d**	sent
len**d**	lent
spen**d**	spent

- Pattern 2: A *-d* or *-t* suffix is added. The vowel changes. (Same as perfect/passive)

feel /fil/	felt /fɛlt/
sleep /slip/	slept /slɛpt/
tell /tɛl/	told /told/

- Pattern 3a: The vowel changes. (Different from perfect/passive)

eat /it/	ate /et/
speak /spik/	spoke /spok/
know /no/	knew /nu/

- Pattern 3b: The vowel changes. (Same as perfect/passive)

hold /hold/	held /hɛld/
meet /mit/	met /mɛt/
sit /sɪt/	sat /sæt/

- Pattern 4: The base form and the simple past form are the same. (Same as perfect/passive)

put	put
hit	hit
cut	cut

exercise   6-1

Complete each sentence with the simple past form of the verb in parentheses. The first five verbs are regular; the second five are irregular.

1. We _____ (work) hard all day.

2. The fans _____ (wait) in line for tickets.

3. I _____ (remember) her face.

4. He _____ (need) a computer upgrade.

5. She _____ (miss) class now and then.

6. They _____ (sell) some of their land.

7. Chen _____ (go) to work at 3:00.

8. Tim and Andrea first _____ (meet) at a mutual friend's party.

9. I accidentally _____ (cut) my finger.

10. Everyone at the party _____ (wear) a costume.

Complete each sentence with either the simple past or the present perfect. Remember that the simple past indicates completion, while the present perfect indicates continued relevance. If you need help, review pages 29–30 and 47.

1. Joe and Donna _____ (live) here in the 1990s.

2. Joe and Donna _____ (live) here since the 1990s.

3. Maria and I _____ (study) together for two years. We meet in the library every Wednesday night at 7:00.

4. Maria and I _____ (study) together last year.

5. We _____ (travel) to London in April.

6. We _____ (travel) to many countries, but this year we're staying home.

7. I _____ (work) for Safeway since May.

8. I _____ (work) for Safeway in 2003.

9. He _____ (build) many houses. He is currently building one on Madison Street.

10. He _____ (build) a house for his sister.

Forming Negatives

To make a verb negative, add the auxiliary verb *did*, which is the simple past form of *do*, and the word *not* before the main verb.

      did not believe

Make each of the following sentences negative.

      EXAMPLE: I made a mistake.
            I did not make a mistake.

1. He came to work on time.

_____

2. My roommate liked the movie.

_____

3. She understood the problem.

   _____

4. We took a wrong turn.

   _____

5. The students needed help with the homework.

   _____

6. The driver blamed me for the accident.

   _____

7. I listened to the directions.

   _____

8. She earned a degree in economics.

   _____

9. He calculated the taxes.

   _____

10. They complained about the weather.

   _____

Forming Contractions

In English, verbs are often combined with other words to form contractions. These shortened forms include an apostrophe (') to indicate missing letters. It is important to learn contractions because you will often hear them in conversation or see them in informal writing. Formal writing, though, rarely contains contractions.

The auxiliary verb *did* is often combined with *not* to form a contraction. Notice that an apostrophe indicates that the letter *o* is omitted:

   did + not = didn't

Rewrite the sentences you wrote in exercise 6-3 using contractions.

1. _____

2. _____

3. _____

4. _____

5. _____

6. _____

7. _____

8. _____

9. _____

10. _____

Forming Yes/No Questions

To form questions that can be answered yes or no (yes/no questions), begin the question with the auxiliary verb *did*. After the auxiliary verb, place the subject and the main verb.

Statement: He took the bus to work.
Yes/no question: Did he take the bus to work?

 **exercise   6-5**

Rewrite the following statements as yes/no questions.

EXAMPLE: You finished your application letter.
Did you finish your application letter?

1. They elected a new president.

   _____

2. She delivered the report.

   _____

3. You expected us earlier.

   _____

4. Tho passed his driver's test.

   _____

5. The committee explored the issues.

   _____

6. He explained the problem.

   _____

7. The director had an appointment at 3:00.

   _____

8. You forgot the map.

   _____

9. The bank lent him some money.

   _____

10. They offered him a job.

   _____

Forming *Wh*-Questions

Wh-questions are used to elicit specific pieces of information. They usually begin with *what, who, why, where, when, how,* or combinations such as *how much, how many,* and *how often.* When the question word is the subject of the sentence, the form of the question is similar to the form of a statement.

> Statement: Someone knocked on the door.
> *Wh*-question: Who knocked at the door?

When the question word is any other part of the sentence, the auxiliary verb *did* comes after the question word and is followed by the subject and the main verb.

> Statement: She bought a new cell phone.
> *Wh*-question: What did she buy?
>
> Statement: They left last night.
> *Wh*-question: When did they leave?

exercise	6-6

Complete the following questions based on the statements provided.

> EXAMPLE: He found the missing document on the top shelf.
> Where *did he find the missing document?*

1. Toni Morrison wrote *Beloved.*

   Who _____

2. Patty won the contest.

   Who _____

3. He turned left.

   Which way _____

4. They traveled to four different countries.

   How many countries _____

5. You taught biology for thirty years.

   How long_____

6. The repair cost $35.00.

   How much_____

7. They stayed at the party until midnight.

   How long_____

8. She ran fifteen miles.

   How far _____

9. They moved to Hong Kong.

   Where _____

10. They climbed to the summit.

    How far _____

Be Verb Forms

The verb *be* has two different forms in the simple past: *was* and *were*.

	Singular	Plural
First Person	I **was**	we **were**
Second Person	you **were**	you **were**
Third Person	he, she, it **was**	they **were**

exercise 7-1

Complete each sentence with the simple past form of the verb be.

1. The test _____ difficult.

2. You _____ right.

3. They _____ envious.

4. Bill _____ ill yesterday.

5. The news _____ good.

6. We _____ embarrassed.

7. I _____ ready for the exam.

8. The keys _____ in the car.

9. It _____ fun.

10. The house _____ old and decrepit.

The word *there* is often used with the verb *be* to acknowledge the existence of someone or something. The form of the verb is based on the subject that follows it.

Singular subject: There **was a storm** last night.
Plural subject: There **were** twelve people in the cast.

Circle the verb that agrees in number with the subject that follows it.

1. There **was/were** a parade yesterday.

2. There **was/were** many celebrities at the rally.

3. There **was/were** a lot of traffic.

4. There **was/were** pizza for everyone.

5. There **was/were** several buildings in need of repair.

6. There **was/were** no more tickets left.

7. There **was/were** a four-hour delay.

8. There **was/were** an empty seat in the back row.

9. There **was/were** many tourists at this year's festival.

10. There **was/were** a nice breeze earlier this morning.

Forming Negatives

To make the verb *be* negative, just add *not*.

was not   were not

Forming Contractions

In conversation and informal writing, you can use contractions.

was not = wasn't   were + not = weren't

Complete the sentences using either wasn't *or* weren't.

1. They _____ at home yesterday.

2. I _____ prepared for such a long trip.

3. There _____ any leftovers.

4. Carlos _____ at work on Tuesday.

5. We _____ pleased with the report.

6. There _____ much time left.

7. Jenny and Sik _____ in class.

8. The lights _____ on.

9. You _____ at the party.

10. The accident _____ serious.

Forming Yes/No Questions

To form yes/no questions, begin the question with a form of the verb *be* and place the subject after it.

Statement: John was late.
Yes/no question: Was John late?

Statement: They were surprised.
Yes/no question: Were they surprised?

To form yes/no questions with *there*, place *there* after the *be* verb.

Statement: There was a message for Natalie on the answering machine.
Yes/no question: Was there a message for Natalie on the answering machine?

 **exercise   7-4**

Rewrite the following statements as questions.

EXAMPLE: He was sick last week.
Was he sick last week?

1. The concert was in the park.

   _____

2. The road was under construction.

   _____

3. Everyone was on time.

   _____

4. The textbooks were expensive.

   _____

5. The job was stressful.

    _____

6. The program was a success.

    _____

7. There were many apartments for rent.

    _____

8. The parking lot was full.

    _____

9. The tickets were free.

    _____

10. The computer was on.

    _____

Forming *Wh*-Questions

To form *wh*-questions, place the *be* verb after the question word. When the question word is the subject of the sentence, the form of the question is similar to the form of a statement.

> Statement: Cindy was the winner.
> *Wh*-question: Who was the winner?

When the question word is any other part of the sentence, the subject follows the *be* verb.

> Statement: They were in Mexico last week.
> *Wh*-question: Where were they last week?

> Statement: She was in the office on Tuesday.
> *Wh*-question: When was she in the office?

 **exercise   7-5**

Complete the following questions based on the statements provided.

> EXAMPLE: The weather was good.
>   How *was the weather?*

1. In 1980, Jimmy Carter was the president of the United States.

    Who _____

2. The trip was long and arduous.

    How _____

3. His grandparents were from Brazil.

   Where _____

4. They were in the library.

   Where _____

5. The field trip was on Wednesday.

   When _____

6. The gym was open four hours on Sunday.

   How long _____

7. CDs and DVDs were on sale.

   What items _____

8. The traffic was bad.

   How _____

9. Seth was there.

   Who _____

10. The movie was two hours long.

    How long _____

Past Progressive (*Be* Verb + *-ing*)

When you refer to a past action, state, or event that is incomplete or in progress, use the past progressive.

> PAST ACTION: In 2002, I **was working** for a large company in Houston.

> PAST STATE: I **was feeling** fine ten minutes ago.

> PAST EVENT: Something strange **was happening**.

A specific time reference is often used with the past progressive. This reference is generally a prepositional phrase or another clause with a simple-past verb form.

> PREPOSITIONAL PHRASE: *By 5:00*, all the participants **were packing** their bags.

> CLAUSE: While I **was preparing** breakfast, *I heard the news on the radio.*

When you want to indicate two simultaneous ongoing actions, use the past progressive for both.

> SIMULTANEOUS ACTIONS: While I **was preparing** breakfast, I **was listening** to the news.

The past progressive consists of the auxiliary verb *be* and the *-ing* form of the main verb. The auxiliary verb is marked for tense.

	Singular	**Plural**
First Person	I **was verb + ing**	we **were verb + ing**
Second Person	you **were verb + ing**	you **were verb + ing**
Third Person	he, she, it **was verb + ing**	they **were verb + ing**

When a one-syllable word or a word with a stressed final syllable ends in a single consonant sound, double the last letter before adding *-ing.*

One-syllable word: swim → swimming

Word ending in a stressed syllable: permit → permitting

BUT show → showing [This word ends in a vowel sound.]

When a word ends with the letter *e*, drop the *e* before adding *-ing*.

 exercise   8-1

Complete each sentence with the past progressive form of the verb in parentheses.

1. The customer _____ (be) rude.

2. The telephone _____ (ring) all day long.

3. While I _____ (wait), I _____ (dream) of distant places.

4. When you visited last year, they _____ (live) in a different apartment.

5. My roommate _____ (take) a nap while I _____ (study).

6. She _____ (put) on her coat when I walked in.

7. Someone _____ (knock) at the door just as I _____ (get) out of bed.

8. It _____ (rain) a few minutes ago.

9. They saw an accident while they _____ (go) to work.

10. We found old books and toys when we _____ (clean).

exercise   8-2

The verb forms in the following sentences are either simple past or past progressive. Decide whether the verb in each sentence indicates a complete action or an ongoing past action. If you need help, review pages 47–48 and 61.

1. He *played* the piano beautifully.

   Complete action   **Action in progress**

2. He *was playing* the piano as the guests were arriving.

   Complete action   **Action in progress**

3. I *was cooking* dinner when I remembered his name.

   Complete action   **Action in progress**

4. I *cooked* dinner for everyone.

   Complete action   **Action in progress**

5. They *were shopping* for a new lamp, but they couldn't find a nice one.

   Complete action   **Action in progress**

6. They *shopped* for a lamp until they found a nice one.

   Complete action   **Action in progress**

7. When we lived in the suburbs, we *commuted* to work.

   Complete action   **Action in progress**

8. While we *were commuting* to work, we talked about our families.

   Complete action   **Action in progress**

9. She *was working* for Apex Law Firm when she received a new job offer.

   Complete action   **Action in progress**

10. She *worked* for Apex Law Firm from 1999 to 2002.

    Complete action   **Action in progress**

Forming Negatives

To make a past progressive verb negative, place *not* after the auxiliary verb.

was not going   were not going

exercise   **8-3**

Make each of the following sentences negative.

EXAMPLE: We were visiting our relatives.
We were not visiting our relatives.

1. He was attending a conference.

   _____

2. They were laughing.

   _____

3. I was complaining about the work.

   _____

4. She was helping us.

_____

5. Ted was studying last night.

_____

6. They were paying attention.

_____

7. I was talking to myself.

_____

8. You were speaking loud enough.

_____

9. They were doing their homework.

_____

10. We were trying hard.

_____

Forming Contractions

Contractions are often formed by combining the auxiliary verb *be* and *not*. You will often hear these contractions in conversation or see them in informal writing, but you will rarely find them used in formal contexts.

Notice that an apostrophe indicates that the letter *o* is omitted:

I wasn't moving   We weren't moving
He wasn't moving   You weren't moving
She wasn't moving   They weren't moving
It wasn't moving

exercise   8-4

Rewrite the sentences in exercise 8-3 using contractions.

1. _____

2. _____

3. _____

4. _____

5. _____

Past Progressive (*Be* Verb + *-ing*)

6. _____

7. _____

8. _____

9. _____

10. _____

Forming Yes/No Questions

To form yes/no questions, begin the question with the auxiliary verb *be*. After the auxiliary verb, place the subject and the *-ing* form of the main verb.

Statement: Prices were dropping.
Yes/no question: Were prices dropping?

exercise   8-5

Rewrite the following statements as yes/no questions.

EXAMPLE: You were singing to yourself.
Were you singing to yourself?

1. The band was giving a free concert.

   _____

2. The light was blinking on and off.

   _____

3. You were watching the championship on television.

   _____

4. They were being careful.

   _____

5. It was snowing all day.

   _____

6. Gabe and Don were singing together.

   _____

7. They were closing the store.

   _____

8. The companies were considering a merger.

   _____

9. They were recycling most of the waste products.

   _____

10. As young children, they were always getting into trouble.

   _____

Forming Wh-Questions

In _wh_-questions, when the question word is the subject of the sentence, the form of the question is similar to the form of a statement.

> Statement: Ken was demanding your attention.
> _Wh_-question: Who was demanding your attention?

When the question word is any other part of the sentence, the auxiliary verb _be_ comes after the question word and is followed by the subject and the _-ing_ form of the main verb.

> Statement: They were going to church.
> _Wh_-question: Where were they going?

> Statement: He was playing solitaire.
> _Wh_-question: What was he playing?

 **exercise   8-6**

Complete the following questions based on the statements provided.

> EXAMPLE: The assistant was making travel arrangements.
> _Who was making travel arrangements?_

1. They were protesting in front of the post office.

   Where _____

2. Carmen was using this computer.

   Who _____

3. You were watching a funny movie on television last night.

   What _____

4. The committee was discussing the new plan.

   What _____

5. The noise was bothering them.

   What _____

6. Lev was spreading rumors.

   Who _____

7. He was working at McDonald's.

   Where _____

8. She was driving seventy-five mph.

   How fast _____

9. He was reading a newspaper during class today.

   What _____

10. They were standing in front of city hall.

    Where _____

Past Perfect

Use the past perfect when you want to refer to a past action, state, or event that occurred prior to another time in the past. The more recent past time may be expressed as a prepositional phrase or as a clause in which another action, state, or event is mentioned.

> PAST ACTION BEFORE PAST TIME: They **had finished** the project *by Friday.*

> PAST STATE BEFORE PAST ACTION: He **had been** depressed *before he went on vacation.*

You can also use the past perfect to refer to a hypothetical action, state, or event.

> HYPOTHETICAL ACTION: If they **had come** earlier, they would have received free tickets.

Sentences such as this one will be discussed in more detail in Part IV.

The past perfect consists of the auxiliary verb *have* and the perfect/passive form of the main verb. The auxiliary verb is marked for past tense. The perfect/passive verb form is used to indicate either the perfect aspect or the passive voice. (The passive voice will be discussed in Part IV.) The perfect/passive form for regular verbs consists of the base form of the verb and the ending *-ed.*

	Singular	Plural
First Person	I **had verb + ed**	we **had verb + ed**
Second Person	you **had verb + ed**	you **had verb + ed**
Third Person	he, she, it **had verb + ed**	they **had verb + ed**

When a one-syllable word or a word with a stressed final syllable ends in a single consonant sound, double the last letter before adding *-ed.*

> One-syllable word: pat → patted

> Word ending in a stressed syllable: occur → occurred

> BUT tow → towed [This word ends in a vowel sound.]

The present/passive forms of irregular verbs can be found in the appendix.

If you would like to see the common patterns that irregular verbs follow, see those listed for the present perfect on pages 29–30.

exercise   9-1

Complete each sentence with the past perfect form of the verb in parentheses. If you need help with irregular verb forms, check the appendix.

1. Before 2001, they _____ (attend) college in Philadelphia.

2. After we _____ (hold) a meeting, we announced our decision.

3. They _____ (sell) most of their furniture before they moved.

4. The employees _____ (meet) the new director already.

5. I _____ (feel) uneasy before I gave my speech.

6. He _____ (hit) twenty home runs before the All-Star Game.

7. We _____ (sit) down right before the concert began.

8. She _____ (run) three marathons by the age of twenty.

9. It _____ (snow) so much that school was canceled.

10. She _____ (be) there so often that everyone knew her.

exercise   9-2

Using the verbs in parentheses, complete each sentence with either the simple past or the past perfect.

1. The taxi _____ (arrive) after he _____ (left).

2. After we _____ (finish) the dishes, we _____ (go) for a walk.

3. The teacher _____ (assign) twenty problems, but most students _____ (complete) only fifteen of them.

4. She _____ (be) tired because she _____ (work) late the night before.

5. He _____ (wear) the ring that his grandfather _____ (give) him.

6. I _____ (revise) a paper that I _____ (write) a year ago.

7. She _____ (knock) on the door before she _____ (enter).

8. All of a sudden we _____ (know) that we _____ (take) the wrong exit off the freeway.

9. He _____ (read) aloud from a new book he _____ (receive) as a gift.

10. They _____ (celebrate) because they _____ (pass) all their classes.

Forming Negatives

To make a past perfect verb negative, place *not* after the auxiliary verb.

had not gone

| exercise | 9-3 |

Complete each of the following sentences with a negative form of the past perfect. Use the subject and verb provided.

EXAMPLE: He, finish
It was midnight, and *he had not finished* his paper.

1. They, meet

_____ before.

2. It, change

Because _____ color, no one could see it.

3. We, consider

_____ all the possibilities.

4. He, want

_____ help from us.

5. She, drive

_____ to the party.

6. You, speak

_____ English before you came here.

7. I, sent

_____ my application in on time.

Forming Contractions

Contractions are often formed by combining pronouns and the auxiliary verb *had* or by combining the auxiliary verb *had* and *not*. You will often hear these contractions in conversation or see them in informal writing, but you will rarely find them used in formal contexts.

Notice that an apostrophe indicates that at least one letter is omitted:

I'd gone	I hadn't gone
You'd gone	You hadn't gone
He'd gone	He hadn't gone
She'd gone	She hadn't gone
It'd gone	It hadn't gone
We'd gone	We hadn't gone
They'd gone	They hadn't gone

exercise	9-4

Rewrite each sentence in exercise 9-3 using a contraction. First, write a positive sentence; then write a negative sentence (with not*).*

EXAMPLE: He, finish
It was midnight, and he'd finished his paper.
It was midnight, and he hadn't finished his paper.

1. _____

_____

2. _____

_____

3. _____

_____

4. _____

_____

5. _____

_____

6. _____

_____

7. _____

_____

Forming Yes/No Questions

To form yes/no questions, begin the question with the auxiliary verb *had*. After the auxiliary verb, place the subject and the perfect/passive form of the main verb.

Statement: She had taught in Mexico before she moved here.
Yes/no question: Had she taught in Mexico before she moved here?

Rewrite the following statements as yes/no questions.

EXAMPLE: He hadn't known about the bad roads before he left.
Hadn't he known about the bad roads before he left?

1. She hadn't called before she arrived.

   _____

2. They hadn't obtained permission before they started the experiment.

   _____

3. Pat had won the first race before he ran the second race.

   _____

4. They had closed the road.

   _____

5. They had canceled the game without prior notice.

   _____

Forming *Wh*-Questions

In *wh*-questions, when the question word is the subject of the sentence, the form of the question is similar to the form of a statement.

Statement: Jackie had not studied English before coming to the United States.
Wh-question: Who had not studied English before coming to the United States?

When the question word is any other part of the sentence, the auxiliary verb *had* comes after the question word and is followed by the subject and the perfect/passive form of the main verb.

Statement: He had walked two miles before he realized his mistake.
Wh-question: How far had he walked before he realized his mistake?

exercise	9-6

Complete the following questions based on the statements provided.

> EXAMPLE: Sharon had worked in Taiwan before she moved to Kuala Lumpur.
>   Where *had Sharon worked before she moved to Kuala Lumpur?*

1. Peggy and Mel had received job offers before they graduated.

   Who _____

2. Peter had broken six track records by the age of eighteen.

   How many track records _____

3. She had taught English for ten years before she went to law school.

   How long _____

4. He had arrived at the gate a minute before the flight attendant closed the door to the plane.

   When _____

5. They had dated for two years before they got married.

   How long _____

Past Perfect Progressive

When you want to refer to an action, a state, or an event that originated prior to another time in the past but is still ongoing or incomplete, use the past perfect progressive.

ONGOING STATE: I **had been having** frequent headaches, so I decided to visit a doctor.

INCOMPLETE ACTION: We **had been making** plans when someone interrupted us.

You can also use the past perfect progressive to refer to a hypothetical action or event.

HYPOTHETICAL ACTION: If they **had been paying** attention, they would have found the clues.

Sentences such as this one will be discussed in more detail in Part IV.

The past perfect progressive consists of two auxiliary verbs, *have* and *be*, and the *-ing* form of the main verb. The auxiliary verb *had* comes first, and it is marked for tense.

Next comes the perfect/passive form of the verb *be—been*. The final element of the past perfect progressive is the *-ing* form of the main verb.

	Singular	Plural
First Person	I **had been verb + ing**	we **had been verb + ing**
Second Person	you **had been verb + ing**	you **had been verb + ing**
Third Person	he, she, it **had been verb + ing**	they **had been verb + ing**

exercise 10-1

Complete each sentence with the past perfect progressive form of the verb in parentheses.

1. I _____ (work) ten-hour days, so I was very tired.

2. We _____ (discuss) that issue when the supervisor walked in.

3. They _____ (study) English since they came in 2001.

4. The company's profits _____ (increase) until they dropped in December.

5. They _____ (play) soccer together for years.

6. It _____ (rain) all day, so the game was postponed.

7. The children _____ (watch) television before we arrived.

8. He _____ (write) newspaper editorials for twenty years.

9. Sally _____ (study) since 6:00 A.M.

10. I _____ (work) for the telephone company before I came here.

Forming Negatives

To make a past perfect progressive verb negative, place *not* after the auxiliary verb *had*.

had not been going

exercise 10-2

Complete each of the following sentences with the negative form of the past perfect progressive. Use the subject and verb provided.

> EXAMPLE: We, expect, not
> *We had not been expecting* your call.

1. The supervisor, assign, not

    _____ much work lately.

2. The weather, improve, not

   _____, so we returned home.

3. Jodi and I, follow, not

   _____ his directions.

4. They, check, not

   _____ the oil in their car frequently enough.

5. She, ignore, not

   _____ the phone messages.

6. You, get, not

   _____ to work on time.

7. I, exercise, not

   _____, so I was feeling sluggish.

Forming Contractions

Contractions are often formed by combining pronouns and the auxiliary verb *had* or by combining the auxiliary verb *had* and *not*. You will often hear these contractions in conversation or see them in informal writing, but you will rarely find them used in formal contexts.

Notice that an apostrophe indicates that at least one letter is omitted:

I'd been going	I hadn't been going
You'd been going	You hadn't been going
He'd been going	He hadn't been going
She'd been going	She hadn't been going
It'd been going	It hadn't been going
We'd been going	We hadn't been going
They'd been going	They hadn't been going

exercise 10-3

Use the pronoun and verb given to create a sentence that contains a contraction. If not *is also given, use a negative contraction.*

   EXAMPLE: We, hope
   We'd been hoping for a nice day.

1. He, expect, not

   _____ a phone call.

2. It, change

   _____ slowly.

3. We, hope

   _____ for good news.

4. They, look, not

   _____ in the right places.

5. She, lie

   _____ on the couch when the doorbell rang.

6. You, joke, not

   _____ about the possible danger.

7. I, think

   _____ about you when your letter arrived.

Forming Yes/No Questions

To form yes/no questions, begin the question with the auxiliary verb *have*. After a tensed form of *have* (*had*), place the subject, the perfect/passive form of the auxiliary verb *be* (*been*), and the *-ing* form of the main verb.

> Statement: She had been doing all her work.
> Yes/no question: Had she been doing all her work?

Rewrite the following statements as yes/no questions.

> EXAMPLE: The administration had been putting pressure on the employees.
> *Had the administration been putting pressure on the employees?*

1. You had been working too hard.

   _____

2. He had been living by himself.

   _____

3. She had been talking too loudly.

   _____

4. They had been waiting a long time.

   _____

5. The suspect had been telling the truth.

   _____

Forming Wh-Questions

In *wh*-questions, when the question word is the subject of the sentence, the form of the question is similar to the form of a statement.

Statement: Joseph had been driving when the accident happened.
Wh-question: Who had been driving when the accident happened?

When the question word is any other part of the sentence, the auxiliary verb *had* comes after the question word and is followed by the subject, the auxiliary verb *been,* and the *-ing* form of the main verb.

Statement: She had been living in St. Louis at the time.
Wh-question: Where had she been living at the time?

exercise   10-5

Complete the following questions based on the statements provided.

EXAMPLE: The band had been playing together for five years.
How long had the band been playing together?

1. Michelle had been making the arrangements.

   Who _____

2. He had been thinking about moving for the last few months.

   How long _____

3. They had been using my old computer before the new shipment arrived.

   What _____

4. Vladimir had been leading the discussion when the argument started.

   Who _____

5. They had been working on the project since June.

   How long _____

Summary of Tense-Aspect Combinations

TENSE/ASPECT	PAST
simple	simple past: *talked*
progressive	past progressive: *was/were talking*
perfect	past perfect: *had talked*
perfect progressive	past perfect progressive: *had been talking*

PART III

THE FUTURE TENSE

Verbs in the future tense occur in four forms, each signaling a different aspect. (*Aspect* is explained in the Introduction.) Each of these forms can be used to predict future actions, states, or events.

SIMPLE FUTURE: I **will work** on my project tomorrow.

FUTURE PROGRESSIVE: I **will be working** for my father next year.

FUTURE PERFECT: By the end of the winter, I **will have worked** here for five years.

FUTURE PERFECT PROGRESSIVE: On Monday, I **will have been working** with you for ten years.

In the following units, you will learn about these verb forms and the reasons for using them.

Simple Future

When you are referring to a future action, state, or event, use the simple future.

> FUTURE ACTION: We **will take** our final exam on Friday.

> FUTURE STATE: They **will be** late.

> FUTURE EVENT: The weather **will improve**.

To form the simple future for both regular and irregular verbs, place the modal auxiliary verb *will* before the base form of the verb.

	Singular	Plural
First Person	I **will verb**	we **will verb**
Second Person	you **will verb**	you **will verb**
Third Person	he, she, it **will verb**	they **will verb**

exercise 11-1

Complete each sentence with the simple future form of the verb in parentheses.

1. We _____ (commute) to work with Megan next year.

2. The project _____ (require) a lot of hard work and patience.

3. I _____ (give) my report on Tuesday.

4. He _____ (visit) his parents this weekend.

5. Dr. Kobashi _____ (be) out of the office next week.

6. They _____ (announce) the winners on the radio.

7. Bob _____ (leave) next month.

8. Lilik and Rebecca _____ (complete) their training in February.

9. I _____ (call) you tomorrow.

10. They _____ (expand) the airport next year.

Forming Contractions: Pronouns with the Auxiliary Verb *Will*

In English, verbs are often combined with other words to form contractions. These shortened forms include an apostrophe (') to indicate missing letters. It is important to learn contractions because you will often hear them in conversation or see them in informal writing. Formal writing, though, rarely contains contractions.

The modal auxiliary verb *will* is often combined with a pronoun to form a contraction. Notice that an apostrophe indicates that the letters *w* and *i* are omitted:

I + will = I'll   we + will = we'll
he + will = he'll   you + will = you'll
she + will = she'll   they + will = they'll
it + will = it'll

 **11-2**

Complete each sentence with a contraction using the pronoun and the verb provided.

EXAMPLE: I, see
I'll see you in the morning.

1. They, believe

   _____ your story.

2. I, deliver

   _____ the package myself.

3. You, like

   _____ their new apartment.

4. It, end

   _____ soon.

5. He, help

   _____ us.

6. She, introduce

   _____ you.

7. We, sit

   _____ together.

Forming Negatives

To form a negative, place *not* between the modal auxiliary verb *will* and the main verb.

will not go

Make each of the following sentences negative.

EXAMPLE: You will find your book over there.
You will not find your book over there.

1. He will finish by tomorrow.

   _____

2. You will have a lot of fun there.

   _____

3. She will know the answer.

   _____

4. We will ignore the problem.

   _____

5. They will keep your secret.

   _____

6. He will lie to you.

   _____

7. I will need help with my homework.

   _____

8. Marian will be alone.

   _____

9. I will mention your name.

   _____

10. They will be late.

    _____

Forming Contractions: *Won't*

In conversation and informal writing, *will* and *not* are often contracted. The letter *i* in *will* changes to *o* in *won't*. The apostrophe indicates that at least one letter is omitted:

will + not = won't

Rewrite the sentences you wrote in exercise 11-3 using contractions.

1. _____

2. _____

3. _____

4. _____

5. _____

6. _____

7. _____

8. _____

9. _____

10. _____

Forming Yes/No Questions

To form questions that can be answered yes or no (yes/no questions), begin the question with the modal auxiliary verb *will*. After the modal verb, place the subject and the main verb.

Statement: You will be away a long time.
Yes/no question: Will you be away a long time?

Rewrite the following statements as yes/no questions.

EXAMPLE: You will know more tomorrow.
Will you know more tomorrow?

1. They will tell us on Friday.

_____

2. She will report the incident.

     _____

3. You will laugh at my mistakes.

     _____

4. Mitch will need some help.

     _____

5. The noise will bother you.

     _____

6. He will lend us some money.

     _____

7. Dr. Silvis will be free at 4:00.

     _____

8. We will meet later.

     _____

9. They will use your plan.

     _____

10. Federal Express will deliver the package to our house.

     _____

Forming *Wh*-Questions

Wh-questions are used to elicit specific pieces of information. They usually begin with *what, who, why, where, when, how,* or combinations such as *how much, how many,* and *how often.* When the question word is the subject of the sentence, the form of the question is similar to the form of a statement.

> Statement: McGraw-Hill will publish his new book.
> *Wh*-question: Who will publish his new book?

When the question word is any other part of the sentence, the auxiliary modal verb *will* comes after the question word, followed by the subject and the main verb.

> Statement: The play will begin at 8:00.
> *Wh*-question: When will the play begin?

> Statement: The package will contain two books and a CD.
> *Wh*-question: What will the package contain?

exercise   11-6

Complete the following questions based on the statements provided.

EXAMPLE: My entire family will be there.
Who *will be there?*

1. His friends will repair his car.

   Who _____

2. The class will meet on Tuesdays and Thursdays

   When _____

3. Rhonda will finish the report by Monday.

   When _____

4. It will cost $30.00.

   How much _____

5. They will blame me for the mistake.

   Whom _____
   (*Who* may be used instead of *whom* in conversation and informal writing.)

6. Professor Johnson and Professor Lee will choose the scholarship winners.

   Who _____

7. The supervisor will be on vacation for two weeks.

   How long _____

8. They will complain about the mess.

   What _____

9. Two students from our class will lead the discussion.

   Who _____

10. The dance group will perform on Thursday.

   When _____

Be Going To

The phrasal modal auxiliary verb *be going to* is also used to indicate future time.

The verb *be* takes three different forms: *am, is,* and *are.*

	Singular	Plural
First Person	I **am going to verb**	we **are going to verb**
Second Person	you **are going to verb**	you **are going to verb**
Third Person	he, she, it **is going to verb**	thcy **are going to verb**

Be going to is less formal than will.

Friend to friend: **I'm going to finish** the project by Friday.

Employee to supervisor: **I'll finish** the project by Friday.

Although sometimes *be going to* and *will* can be used interchangeably, there are two special uses. *Be going to* signals that something is imminent.

The alarm **is going to sound** in a second.

Will is used to make commitments.

I'll meet you at 5:00.

You will learn more about modal auxiliary verbs in Part V.

exercise | **12-1**

Complete each sentence with a form of be going to *and the main verb.*

1. This job _____ (be) difficult.

2. Our neighbors _____ (build) a new garage.

3. My roommate _____ (buy) a new printer.

4. I _____ (cancel) my magazine subscription.

5. Members of the Outing Club _____ (climb) Mt. Hood.

6. We _____ (celebrate) tonight.

7. He _____ (call) me today.

8. Matt _____ (come) over this evening.

9. Someone from the firm _____ (deliver) the letter tomorrow.

10. They _____ (elect) a new prime minister this year.

 **exercise   12-2**

Complete each sentence with either will *or a form of* be going to. *Circle the reason that supports your answer.*

1. Watch out. It _____ fall.

   Imminent action   **Commitment**

2. I _____ work for you on Friday.

   Imminent action   **Commitment**

3. I _____ sit down right now.

   Imminent action   **Commitment**

4. Sit down. The movie _____ start.

   Imminent action   **Commitment**

5. Beth and I _____ help you next week.

   Imminent action   **Commitment**

Forming Negatives

To make the phrasal modal verb *be going to* negative, just add *not* after *be*.

am not going to   is not going to   are not going to

exercise 12-3

Complete each of the following sentences using a negative form of be going to *and the subject and verb provided.*

> EXAMPLE: He, accept
> He *is not going to accept* the job offer.

1. Taxes, increase

   _____ this year.

2. It, snow

   _____ tonight.

3. We, go

   _____ to the party.

4. He, listen

   _____ to your advice.

5. She, travel

   _____ alone.

6. You, have

   _____ enough time.

7. I, forget

   _____ you.

Forming Contractions

Contractions are often formed by combining pronouns and the verb *be* or by combining the verb *be* and *not*. You will often hear these contractions in conversation or see them in informal writing, but you will rarely find them used in formal contexts.

Notice that an apostrophe indicates that a letter is omitted:

I'm going to	I'm not going to	
You're going to	You're not going to	You aren't going to
He's going to	He's not going to	He isn't going to
She's going to	She's not going to	She isn't going to
It's going to	It's not going to	It isn't going to
We're going to	We're not going to	We aren't going to
They're going to	They're not going to	They aren't going to

Complete the following sentences using contractions. For some sentences more than one form can be used.

> EXAMPLE: He, appear
> *He's going to appear* on television this evening.

1. He, come, not

   _____ with us.

2. It, rain

   _____ soon.

3. I, clean

   _____ my room tonight.

4. They, believe, not

   _____ your story.

5. She, call, not

   _____ tonight.

6. You, do

   _____ well on the exam.

7. I, cook, not

   _____ anything special.

Forming Yes/No Questions

To form yes/no questions, begin the question with a form of the verb *be* and the subject.

> Statement: They are going to win.
> Yes/no question: Are they going to win?

Rewrite the following statements as questions.

> EXAMPLE: He is going to design a new line of clothing.
> *Is he going to design a new line of clothing?*

1. They are going to consider your proposal.

   _____

2. You are going to enter the park at the north gate.

   _____

3. The doctor is going to explain the procedure.

   _____

4. We are going to explore our new neighborhood today.

   _____

5. He's going to fix it for free.

   _____

6. You are going to follow us.

   _____

7. She's going to get into trouble.

   _____

8. It's going to happen soon.

   _____

9. He's going to like this idea.

   _____

10. We're going to look for a new apartment today.

    _____

Forming *Wh*-Questions

In *wh*-questions, when a question word is the subject of a sentence, the form of the question is similar to the form of a statement.

> Statement: Judy is going to assist us.
> *Wh*-question: Who is going to assist us?

When the question word is any other part of the sentence, place a form of the verb *be* and the subject after the question word.

> Statement: They are going to leave next week.
> *Wh*-question: When are they going to leave?

> Statement: He is going to park the car in the corner lot.
> *Wh*-question: Where is he going to park the car?

exercise	12-6

Complete the following questions based on the statements provided.

> EXAMPLE: They are going to cut costs by closing some plants.
> How *are they going to cut costs?*

1. My cousin is going to move to Chile.

   Who _____

2. She is going to earn $10.00 an hour.

   How much _____

3. We are going to eat late tonight.

   When _____

4. They are going to improve the roads this year.

   When _____

5. You are going to develop the film tomorrow.

   When _____

6. They are going to invite everyone in the neighborhood.

   Whom _____
   (*Who* may be used instead of *whom* in conversation and informal writing.)

7. The legislators are going to discuss the bill on Friday.

   When _____

8. He is going to live in Tokyo.

   Where _____

9. My daughter is going to march in the parade.

   Who _____

10. The eclipse is going to occur on Saturday.

    When _____

Future Progressive (*Will Be* Verb + *-ing*)

Use the future progressive when you refer to an action or event that will be ongoing at some time or for some period of time in the future.

> FUTURE ACTION OCCURRING FOR A PERIOD OF TIME: I **will be studying** all night.

> FUTURE EVENT OCCURRING AT A POINT IN TIME: *At approximately 7:30*, the sun **will be sinking** behind the horizon.

The future progressive consists of the auxiliary verbs *will* and *be* and the *-ing* form of the main verb.

	Singular	**Plural**
First Person	I **will be verb + ing**	we **will be verb + ing**
Second Person	you **will be verb + ing**	you **will be verb + ing**
Third Person	he, she, it **will be verb + ing**	they **will be verb + ing**

When a one-syllable word or a word with a stressed final syllable ends in a single consonant sound, double the last letter before adding *-ing*.

> One-syllable word: plan → planning

> Word ending in a stressed syllable: emit → emitting

> BUT sew → sewing [This word ends in a vowel sound.]

When a word ends with a consonant and the letter *e*, drop the *e* before adding *-ing*: come → coming. The letter *e* is not dropped from words such as *be*, *see*, and *free*.

exercise   13-1

Complete each sentence with the future progressive form of the verb in parentheses.

1. Sean _____ (represent) us at the meeting.

2. They _____ (leave) at 6:00.

3. Their car _____ (follow) ours.

4. We _____ (wait) for you on the corner.

5. He _____ (watch) the clock.

6. They _____ (produce) more energy than they need.

7. The tour company _____ (provide) lunch.

8. It _____ (snow) in the mountains.

9. Look for me by the entry. I _____ (wear) a red hat.

10. The Copy Shop _____ (open) a new store downtown this year.

Forming Negatives

To make a future progressive verb negative, place *not* after *will.*

   will not be flying

exercise   13-2

Complete each of the following sentences with a negative form of the future progressive. Use the subject and verb provided.

   EXAMPLE: I, attend
            I will not be attending the meeting.

1. They, appear

    _____ on television.

2. It, start

    _____ on time.

3. We, read

    _____ that novel this term.

4. He, arrive

_____ in time for the party.

5. She, stay

_____ in a hotel.

6. You, live

_____ by yourself.

7. I, make

_____ much money next year.

Forming Contractions

Contractions are often formed by combining pronouns and the auxiliary verb *will* or by combining the auxiliary verb *will* and *not*. You will often hear these contractions in conversation or see them in informal writing, but you will rarely find them used in formal contexts.

Remember that an apostrophe indicates that at least one letter is omitted and that the letter *i* in *will* changes to *o* in the negative contraction *won't*:

I'll be working	I won't be working
You'll be working	You won't be working
He'll be working	He won't be working
She'll be working	She won't be working
It'll be working	It won't be working
We'll be working	We won't be working
They'll be working	They won't be working

exercise   13-3

Use the pronoun and verb given to create a sentence that contains a contraction. If not *is also given, use a negative contraction.*

EXAMPLE: She, come, not
She won't be coming to the party.

1. He, joining, not

_____ us this evening.

2. It, affect

_____ everyone.

3. I, treat

_____ for dinner tonight.

4. They, need, not

   _____ any more help.

5. She, arrive, not

   _____ until midnight.

6. You, fly

   Tomorrow _____ to Honolulu.

7. I, think, not

   _____ of much besides the exam.

Forming Yes/No Questions

To form yes/no questions, begin the question with the auxiliary verb *will*. Follow *will* with the subject, *be*, and the *-ing* form of the main verb.

> Statement: He will be coming along.
> Yes/no question: Will he be coming along?

Rewrite the following statements as yes/no questions.

> EXAMPLE: She will be playing for our team this year.
> *Will she be playing for our team this year?*

1. I will be seeing you next week.

   _____

2. They will be traveling by bus.

   _____

3. Takamitsu will be assisting Heather.

   _____

4. They will be offering special packages at the end of the season.

   _____

5. You will be checking your e-mail daily.

   _____

Forming *Wh*-Questions

In *wh*-questions, when a question word is the subject of the sentence, the form of the question is similar to the form of a statement.

      Statement: Debbie Little will be running for office next year.
      Wh-question: Who will be running for office next year?

When the question word is any other part of the sentence, the auxiliary verb *will* comes after the question word and is followed by the subject, *be*, and the *-ing* form of the main verb.

      Statement: They will be playing soccer on Sunday.
      Wh-question: When will they be playing soccer?

 **exercise   13-5**

Complete the questions below based on the statements provided.

    EXAMPLE: Alison will be accompanying them.
             Who *will be accompanying them?*

1. Kenji will be taking notes.

    Who _____

2. The star of the show will be receiving an award.

    Who _____

3. They will be sitting in the back row.

    Where _____

4. You will be driving two hundred miles on your first day.

    How far _____

5. She will be finishing her project in May.

    When _____

Future Perfect

Use the future perfect when you want to refer to a future action, state, or event that will be completed by a specific time in the future.

> FUTURE ACTION: *By next week*, she **will have completed** the course.

> FUTURE STATE: *In 2005*, we **will have known** each other for twenty years.

> FUTURE EVENT: The ship **will have sunk** *by then*.

The future perfect consists of the modal auxiliary verb *will*, the auxiliary verb *have*, and the perfect/passive form of the main verb. The perfect/passive verb form is used to indicate either the perfect aspect or the passive voice. (The passive voice will be discussed in Part IV.) The perfect/passive form for regular verbs consists of the base form of the verb and the ending *-ed*.

	Singular	**Plural**
First Person	I **will have verb + ed**	we **will have verb + ed**
Second Person	you **will have verb + ed**	you **will have verb + ed**
Third Person	he, she, it **will have verb + ed**	they **will have verb + ed**

When a one-syllable word or a word with a stressed final syllable ends in a single consonant sound, double the last letter before adding *-ed*.

> One-syllable word: flip → flipped

> Word ending in a stressed syllable: refer → referred

> BUT bow → bowed [This word ends in a vowel sound.]

The perfect/passive forms of irregular verbs can be found in the appendix.

If you would like to see the common patterns irregular verbs follow, see those listed for the present perfect on pages 29–30.

 **exercise   14-1**

Complete each sentence with the future perfect form of the verb in parentheses. If you need help with irregular verb forms, check the appendix.

1. By the time you arrive, most guests _____ (leave).

2. I _____ (write) the report by the time you get here.

3. By 10:00 A.M., all the participants _____ (introduce) themselves.

4. By the time they reach Sydney, they _____ (fly) four thousand miles.

5. We _____ (eat) dinner by the time they get here.

Forming Negatives

To make a future perfect verb negative, place *not* after *will.*

will not have gone

exercise   14-2

Make each sentence negative. Be sure to use the subject and the future perfect form of the verb provided.

EXAMPLE: admit

By the time he's ninety years old, he still *will not have admitted* his mistake.

1. You, rest

    _____ before you meet the chair of the committee.

2. They, eat

    By the end of the fast, they _____ for twenty-four hours.

3. We, finish

    _____ our lunch by the time she arrives.

4. Mark, sleep

    _____ much before he makes his presentation.

5. She, save

    _____ enough money for college by the time classes begin.

Forming Contractions

Contractions are often formed by combining pronouns and the auxiliary verb *will* or by combining the auxiliary verb *will* and *not*. You will often hear these contractions in conversation or see them in informal writing, but you will rarely find them used in formal contexts.

Remember that an apostrophe indicates that at least one letter is omitted and that the letter *i* in *will* changes to *o* in the negative contraction *won't*:

I'll have moved	I won't have moved
You'll have moved	You won't have moved
He'll have moved	He won't have moved
She'll have moved	She won't have moved
It'll have moved	It won't have moved
We'll have moved	We won't have moved
They'll have moved	They won't have moved

exercise 14-3

Use the pronoun and verb given to create a sentence that contains a contraction. If not *is also given, use a negative contraction.*

> EXAMPLE: It, change
> By next year, *it'll have changed.*

1. They, complete

   By the time the director arrives, _____ the report.

2. He, finish, not

   By the time I return, _____ the work.

3. You, recover

   By the end of May, _____ completely.

4. They, make, not

   _____ much progress without our help.

5. She, give

   _____ the job to someone else by the time my application arrives.

Forming Yes/No Questions

To form yes/no questions, begin the question with the auxiliary verb *will*, following it with the subject, *have*, and the perfect/passive form of the main verb.

> Statement: You will have completed your coursework by May.
> Yes/no question: Will you have completed your coursework by May?

exercise   14-4

Rewrite the following statements as yes/no questions.

> EXAMPLE: They will have discussed the issue by the time we arrive.
> *Will they have discussed the issue by the time we arrive?*

1. The landscape will have changed by the time he's an adult.

   _____

2. By July 11, we will have made our decision.

   _____

3. By the time you start your new job, you will have finished your degree.

   _____

4. By the time we get home, he will have called already.

   _____

5. When we get to the movie theater, the movie will have started already.

   _____

Forming *Wh*-Questions

In *wh*-questions, when the question word is the subject of the sentence, the form of the question is similar to the form of a statement.

> Statement: Bruce will have resigned by the time the scandal appears in newspapers.
> *Wh*-question: Who will have resigned by the time the scandal appears in newspapers?

When the question word is any other part of the sentence, the auxiliary verb *will* comes after the question word, followed by the auxiliary verb *have*, the subject, and the perfect/passive form of the main verb.

> Statement: By the time you're fifty years old, you will have worked at the firm for twenty-five years.
> *Wh*-question: How long will you have worked for the firm by the time you're fifty years old?

exercise   14-5

Complete the following questions based on the statements provided.

> EXAMPLE: She will have received her results by the time she leaves our office.
> When *will she have received her results?*

1. By the end of the season, Nat will have become the record holder.

   By the end of the season, who _____

2. She will have lived in Moscow three months when her family arrives.

   How long _____

3. By the time he's thirty, Andy will have run sixteen marathons.

   By the time he's thirty, how many marathons _____

4. By the time it is built, they will have spent more than a million dollars.

   By the time it is built, how much _____

5. When his new book comes out, he will have written ten novels.

   When his new book comes out, how many novels _____

Future Perfect Progressive

When you want to refer to an ongoing action, state, or event or to a habitual action that will continue until or through a specific time, use the future perfect progressive.

> HABITUAL ACTION: *In October,* we **will have been commuting** together for twenty years.

> ONGOING EVENT: *By that time,* the temperature **will have been increasing** steadily for five years.

The future perfect progressive consists of three auxiliary verbs—*will, have,* and *be*—and the *-ing* form of the main verb. The auxiliary verbs *will* and *have* come first. Next is the perfect/passive form of the verb *be*—*been.* The final element of the future perfect progressive is the *-ing* form of the main verb.

	Singular	**Plural**
First Person	I **will have been verb + ing**	we **will have been verb + ing**
Second Person	you **will have been verb + ing**	you **will have been verb + ing**
Third Person	he, she, it **will have been verb + ing**	they will **have been verb + ing**

exercise | **15-1**

Complete each sentence with the future perfect progressive form of the verb in parentheses.

1. In December, we _____ (live) in this house for ten years.

2. By the time of our next meeting, we _____ (discuss) this plan for three years.

3. By the time of the recital, I _____ (practice) four hours a day, seven days a week.

4. When the Mariners meet the Red Sox, they _____ (play) on the road for six days already.

5. In June, they _____ (work) together for thirty years.

Forming Negatives

To make a future perfect progressive verb negative, place *not* after the auxiliary verb *will*.

will not have been going

exercise 15-2

Complete each of the following sentences with a negative form of the future perfect progressive. Use the subject and verb provided.

EXAMPLE: He, answer, not
By the end of today, *he will not have been answering* his phone for a week.

1. They, talk, not

By Thursday, _____ to each other for a week.

2. The subways, run, not

By the end of the strike, _____ for six days.

3. They, produce, not

In January, _____ that type of car for three years.

4. The dance troupe, perform, not

At the end of the December, _____ for a whole year.

5. She, work, not

On Monday, _____ for three months.

Forming Contractions

Contractions are often formed by combining pronouns and the auxiliary verb *will* or by combining the auxiliary verb *will* and *not*. You will often hear these contractions in conversation or see them in informal writing, but you will rarely find them used in formal contexts.

Remember that an apostrophe indicates that at least one letter is omitted and that the letter *i* in *will* changes to *o* in the negative contraction *won't*:

I'll have been going   I won't have been going
You'll have been going   You won't have been going
He'll have been going   He won't have been going

She'll have been going
It'll have been going
We'll have been going
They'll have been going

She won't have been going
It won't have been going
We won't have been going
They won't have been going

exercise	15-3

Use the pronoun and verb given to create a sentence that contains a contraction. If not *is also given, use a negative contraction.*

> EXAMPLE: The foundation, donate
> By next year, the foundation *will have been donating* money to that organization for five years.

1. They, work, not

   By the end of February, _____ the same shift for two months.

2. They, broadcast

   By the end of this year, _____ for fifty years.

3. We, rent

   On Friday, _____ _____ this apartment for ten years.

4. They, return

   In June, _____ to the same place every summer for ten years.

5. He, assist, not

   By the end of this month, _____ us for a full year.

Forming *Wh*-Questions

In *wh*-questions, when the question word is the subject of the sentence, the form of the question is similar to the form of a statement.

> Statement: When the project is finished, Cheryl will have been working more than anybody else.
> *Wh*-question: When the project is finished, who will have been working more than anybody else?

When the question word is any other part of the sentence, the auxiliary verb *will* comes after the question word and is followed by the subject, the auxiliary verbs *have been*, and the *-ing* form of the main verb.

> Statement: By the end of December, they will have been doing business together for twenty-five years.
> *Wh*-question: By the end of the year, how long will they have been doing business together?

exercise   15-4

Complete the following questions based on the statements provided.

> EXAMPLE: At the end of the summer, the band will have been playing together for five years.
> At the end of the summer, how long *will the band have been playing together?*

1. By the end of June, Anne and Derrick will have been making the schedule for five years.

   By the end of June, who _____

2. By Friday, the dance contestants will have been dancing for seventy-two hours.

   By Friday, how long _____

3. By the end of July, we will have been using this computer for ten years.

   By the end of July, how long _____

4. By Saturday, you will have been working on this paper for a whole month.

   By Saturday, how long _____

5. By the end of the year, Ron will have been keeping a journal for five years.

   By the end of the year, how long _____

Summary of Tense-Aspect Combinations

TENSE/ASPECT	FUTURE
simple	simple future: *will talk*
progressive	future progressive: *will be talking*
perfect	future perfect: *will have talked*
perfect progressive	future perfect progressive: *will have been talking*

PART IV

IMPERATIVE, PASSIVE, AND HYPOTHETICAL CONDITIONAL

As you read the units that follow, you will learn to use verbs in three special constructions: the imperative, the passive, and the hypothetical conditional.

IMPERATIVE: Be careful!

PASSIVE: We were surprised by the news.

HYPOTHETICAL CONDITIONAL: If I were you, I would look for a new job.

Imperative

When you want to give instructions or directions, you can use the imperative:

INSTRUCTION: **Mix** the ingredients together.

DIRECTION: **Turn** right at the corner.

Imperatives are used for other purposes as well:

REQUEST: **Close** the window, please.

WARNING: **Watch** out!

INVITATION: **Come** over to our house tonight.

WISH: **Have** a nice time.

Using the verb in the imperative construction is easy because there are no endings. Just use the base form (the form found in the dictionary).

Because imperatives are directed toward another person or other persons, the subject *you* is understood; that is, it is not mentioned except for emphasis.

exercise   16-1

Choose a verb from the list to complete the imperative sentences.

answer	bake	be	call	drive
finish	have	meet	open	turn

1. Please _____ the telephone.

2. _____ a nice weekend.

3. _____ the door, please.

4. Please _____ quiet.

5. _____ your work by Friday.

6. _____ an ambulance!

7. _____ the cookies for fifteen minutes.

8. _____ me in the hotel lobby.

9. _____ left at the corner.

10. _____ safely.

Forming Negatives

To form a negative imperative, place the auxiliary verb *do* and the word *not* before the base form of the verb.

> do not go

Forming Contractions: *Don't*

In informal or conversational situations, use a contraction.

> don't go

exercise   16-2

Complete the following sentences using the negative form of the verb provided. Then rewrite the sentence using a contraction.

EXAMPLE: walk
> *Do not walk* on the grass.
> *Don't walk* on the grass.

1. Be

_____ late!

_____

2. Run

_____ on the deck of the pool.

_____

3. Forget

_____ your homework.

_____

4. Lie

_____ to me.

_____

5. Shout

_____ at us.

_____

6. Drink

_____ the water.

_____

7. Start

_____ the car yet.

_____

8. Blame

_____ me.

_____

9. Boil

_____ the water too long.

_____

10. Break

_____ anything.

_____

Forming Contractions: *Let's*

The contraction *let's* (for *let us*) is often used to make suggestions.

Let's go to the movies.
Let's not wait any longer.

The uncontracted form is used only in very formal situations—religious ceremonies, for example.

Let us join together in prayer.

exercise   16-3

Use let's *or* let's not *to complete the following sentences. Use the verb provided.*

1. make

   _____ something easy for dinner.

2. forget, not

   _____ the tickets.

3. stay, not

   _____ at the party very late.

4. call

   _____ Anna and Charlie.

5. celebrate

   _____ tonight.

Passive

The sentences that you studied in Parts I through III were in the active voice. Most of them had subjects that performed actions. In contrast, sentences in the passive voice have subjects that receive some action.

ACTIVE: **George Lucas** produced the film.

PASSIVE: **The film** was produced by George Lucas.

In passive sentences, the doer of the action is sometimes in a prepositional phrase starting with the preposition *by*, as in "by George Lucas." In other instances, there is no *by* phrase because the doer of the action is not important or is not known.

Microcomputers were used in the study.

In passive sentences, the main verb is in the perfect/passive form. You have already studied this form in Parts I, II, and III. To refresh your memory, see pages 29–30, 69, and 101. The auxiliary *be* precedes the perfect/passive form of the main verb.

Oranges **are grown** in Florida.

In the present tense, regular verbs follow this pattern:

	Singular	Plural
First Person	I **am verb + ed**	we **are verb + ed**
Second Person	you **are verb + ed**	you **are verb + ed**
Third Person	he, she, it **is verb + ed**	they **are verb + ed**

Contracted forms: *I'm, you're, he's, she's, it's, we're, they're*

The pattern for regular verbs in the past tense is as follows:

	Singular	Plural
First Person	I **was verb + ed**	we **were verb +ed**
Second Person	you **were verb + ed**	you **were verb + ed**
Third Person	he, she, it **was verb + ed**	they **were verb + ed**

No contracted forms

Both the modal verb *will* and the auxiliary verb *be* are used to signal the future:

	Singular	Plural
First Person	I **will be verb + ed**	we **will be verb + ed**
Second Person	you **will be verb + ed**	you **will be verb + ed**
Third Person	he, she, it **will be verb + ed**	they **will be verb + ed**

Contracted forms: *I'll, you'll, he'll, she'll, it'll, we'll, you'll, they'll*

For the perfect/passive forms of irregular verbs, consult the appendix.

exercise   17-1

Complete each passive sentence with the form of the verb indicated in parentheses. Then rewrite the sentence using a pronoun and, if possible, a contraction.

EXAMPLE: The experiment *will be performed* (perform, future) tomorrow.
It'll be performed tomorrow.

1. James _____ (reward, future) for his work.

   _____

2. The students _____ (affect, past) by the changes in the tax law.

   _____

3. Newspapers _____ (deliver, present) daily.

   _____

4. Potatoes _____ (grow, present) in Idaho.

   _____

5. The winners _____ (announce, past) yesterday.

   _____

6. Your schedules _____ (change, future) next week.

   _____

7. The soccer match _____ (reschedule, future).

   _____

8. All the students in class _____ (invite, present) to the party.

   _____

9. Carmen _____ (blame, past) for the error.

   _____

10. The house _____ (destroy, past).

   _____

Progressive Verbs in the Passive Voice

Progressive verbs in the passive voice have an additional auxiliary verb *be*, which has the progressive *-ing* ending: *being*.

Present progressive verbs in the passive voice follow this pattern:

	Singular	Plural
First Person	I **am being verb + ed**	we **are being verb +ed**
Second Person	you **are being verb + ed**	you **are being verb + ed**
Third Person	he, she, it **is being verb + ed**	they **are being verb + ed**

Contracted forms: *I'm, you're, he's, she's, it's, we're, they're*

Past progressive verbs are similar, but the tense of the first auxiliary *be* changes:

	Singular	Plural
First Person	I **was being verb + ed**	we **were being verb + ed**
Second Person	you **were being verb + ed**	you **were being verb + ed**
Third Person	he, she, it **was being verb + ed**	they **were being verb + ed**

No contracted forms

The future progressive is rarely used, so it will not be presented here.

 **exercise**   **17-2**

Complete each passive sentence with the form of the verb indicated in parentheses. Then rewrite the sentence using a pronoun and, if possible, a contraction.

> EXAMPLE: A new rocket *is being designed* (design, present progressive).
> *It's being designed.*

1. This event _____ (broadcast, present progressive) around the world.

   _____

2. New uses for recycled materials _____ (develop, present progressive).

   _____

3. The luggage _____ (carry, past progressive) to the plane when one of the suitcases popped open.

   _____

4. The issues _____ (discuss, past progressive) when we arrived.

   _____

5. Your job application _____ (consider, present progressive).

   _____

6. Our passports _____ (check, past progressive) when the alarm rang.

_____

7. New council members _____ (elect, present progressive) this year.

_____

8. That store _____ (close, present progressive) because of safety problems.

_____

9. The protestors _____ (ignore, past progressive) by the politicians.

_____

10. Donations _____ (collect, present progressive) for the poor.

_____

Perfect Verbs in the Passive Voice

Perfect verbs in the passive voice have two auxiliary verbs—*have*, which carries tense, and *be*, which is in the perfect/passive form *been*.

Present perfect verbs in the passive voice follow this pattern:

	Singular	Plural
First Person	I **have been verb + ed**	we **have been verb + ed**
Second Person	you **have been verb + ed**	you **have been verb + ed**
Third Person	he, she, it **has been verb + ed**	they **have been verb + ed**

Contracted forms: *I've, you've, he's, she's, it's, we've, they've*

Past perfect verbs are similar, but the form of the first auxiliary changes to *had* to indicate the past tense:

	Singular	Plural
First Person	I **had been verb + ed**	we **had been verb + ed**
Second Person	you **had been verb + ed**	you **had been verb + ed**
Third Person	he, she, it **had been verb + ed**	they **had been verb + ed**

Contracted forms: *I'd, you'd, he'd, she'd, it'd, we'd, they'd*

Future perfect verbs include the modal verb *will*, as well as the auxiliaries *have* and *be*:

	Singular	Plural
First Person	I **will have been verb + ed**	we **will have been verb + ed**
Second Person	you **will have been verb + ed**	you **will have been verb + ed**
Third Person	he, she, it **will have been verb + ed**	they **will have been verb + ed**

Perfect progressive verbs in the passive voice are extremely rare; they will not be presented here.

exercise   17-3

Complete each passive sentence with the form of the verb indicated in parentheses. Then rewrite the sentence using a pronoun and, if possible, a contraction.

EXAMPLE: The lost information *has been retrieved.* (retrieve, present perfect).
It's been retrieved.

1. My brother _____ (promote, present perfect).

    _____

2. The jobs _____ (assign, future perfect) by the time we arrive.

    _____

3. My parents _____ (delay, past perfect) at the airport, so they were late.

    _____

4. The work _____ (finish, future perfect) when the director meets with us.

    _____

5. Her first book _____ (praised, past perfect) highly.

    _____

6. Amy and I _____ (notify, future perfect) of any problems before we leave.

    _____

7. The arrangements _____ (make, present perfect).

    _____

8. The job _____ (offer, present perfect) to Laila.

    _____

9. The report _____ (revise, present perfect).

    _____

10. The roads _____ (improve, past perfect) since my previous visit.

    _____

Forming Negatives

To form a negative sentence, place the word *not* after the first auxiliary verb.

Examples: is not spoken, is not being written, has not been read, will not have been noticed

exercise   17-4

Make each of the following sentences negative.

  EXAMPLE: The cause of the fire was discovered.
     The cause of the fire was not discovered.

1. The game was canceled.

  _____

2. Rita has been fired.

  _____

3. By this time next year, the project will have been completed.

  _____

4. Some of the important issues are being discussed.

  _____

5. Our bags are being searched.

  _____

6. Your x-rays will be returned to you.

  _____

7. The recent findings are being presented to the public.

  _____

8. The cell phone had been taken from the car.

  _____

9. This computer has been used before.

  _____

10. The document is being prepared by the secretary.

  _____

Forming Questions

  Passive questions are formed in two ways. For yes/no questions and for *wh*-questions in which the question word is not the subject, the first (or only) auxiliary verb begins the question and is followed by the subject.

    Has the letter been sent?
    When will the letter be sent?

When the question word is the subject, it begins the question and is followed by the auxiliary and main verbs.

What was sent?

exercise 17-5

Rewrite the following statements as yes/no questions.

EXAMPLE: The report was revised.
Was the report revised?

1. All questions were answered.

   _____

2. Everyone has been notified of the cancellation.

   _____

3. The basketball game will be broadcast.

   _____

4. The road is being repaired.

   _____

5. Enough evidence had been collected.

   _____

6. He was impressed by the report.

   _____

7. The costs for the project have been calculated.

   _____

8. Jobs are being cut.

   _____

9. Solutions to the problem are being explored.

   _____

10. The clock will be fixed tomorrow.

    _____

exercise   17-6

Complete the following questions based on the statements provided.

EXAMPLE: His car was stolen.
What *was stolen?*

1. Catherine Haley has been elected.

   Who _____

2. The cave was explored.

   What _____

3. Shoshona was given a scholarship.

   Who _____

4. Pineapple is grown in Hawaii.

   What _____

5. My old teacher is being honored at the special dinner tonight.

   Who _____

6. The invitations are being sent on Friday.

   When _____

7. The books were moved to the new library last year.

   When _____

8. The new lights are being installed in all the classrooms.

   Where _____

9. Thirty-two credits are required for graduation.

   How many credits _____

10. The furniture was damaged in the fire.

   What _____

Hypothetical Conditional

The sentences you will study in this unit have two parts: an *if* clause and a main clause. The *if* clause consists of a condition that is either slightly possible or impossible; the main clause states the consequences of the condition mentioned in the *if* clause.

> SLIGHTLY POSSIBLE: If he felt better, he would come with us.

> IMPOSSIBLE: If my aunt were still alive, she would be a hundred years old today.

To form a hypothetical conditional that refers to present or future time, use the simple past tense in the *if* clause; use a modal verb (either *would*, *might*, or *could*) and the base form of the main verb in the main clause.

> If he **studied** more, he **would earn** better grades.

In formal English, *were* is used in the *if* clause, even following the first- and third-person singular pronouns.

> If I **were** you, I would look for a job.

> If she **were** here, we could leave.

To form a hypothetical conditional that refers to past time, use the past perfect in the *if* clause; use *would have*, *might have*, or *could have* and the perfect/passive form of the main verb in the main clause.

> If they **had asked** earlier, I **could have** helped them.

exercise	18-1

Complete each conditional sentence with the correct form of the verb in parentheses. Each sentence refers to either present or future time. In the main clause, use would *before the base form of the verb.*

1. If I _____ (be) the director, I _____ (change) the policy.

2. If you _____ (check) your e-mail more often, you _____ (know) about the assignments.

3. If we _____ (commute) together, the drive _____ (cost) less.

4. If he _____ (have) more time, he _____ (go) to the game with us.

5. If Emma _____ (visit) us on Thursday, she _____ (meet) my sisters.

6. If you _____ (mail) the package today, they _____ (receive) it by Friday.

7. If they _____ (lower) their prices, more people _____ (shop) there.

8. If we _____ (earn) more money, we _____ (buy) a new car.

9. If he _____ (exercise) more frequently, he _____ (be) healthier.

10. If my grandfather _____ (be) here, he _____ (tell) a joke.

exercise   18-2

Complete each conditional sentence with the correct form of the verb in parentheses. Each sentence refers to past time. In the main clause, use would have *before the perfect/passive form of the verb.*

1. If it _____ (rain), they _____ (cancel) the game.

2. If you _____ (be) on the roller coaster, you _____ (be) sick.

3. If I _____ (know) about the detour, I _____ (take) another route.

4. If she _____ (follow) the directions, she _____ (be) on time.

5. If I _____ (study) harder, I _____ (pass) the exam.

6. If he _____ (be) more productive, he _____ (receive) a promotion.

7. If they _____ (raise) tuition, the students _____ (protest).

8. If they _____ (repair) the car yesterday, we _____ (leave) today.

9. If you _____ (revise) your paper, your main points _____ (be) clearer.

10. If I _____ (be) the manager, I _____ (hire) Yoshi.

PART V

PHRASAL VERBS AND MODAL AUXILIARY VERBS

As you study the units that follow, you will learn about two special types of verbs: phrasal verbs and modal auxiliary verbs. Phrasal verbs are verb-particle combinations, such as *look up* in *I'll look up his phone number*. Modal auxiliary verbs are auxiliaries that signal such meanings as obligation and possibility. Although you have been introduced to modal auxiliary verbs in previous units (*will* and *would*, for example), in Part V you will learn more about the subtle shades of meaning that tense and aspect add to these verbs.

Phrasal Verbs

Phrasal verbs are combinations of verbs and particles. Common particles include *in*, *on*, *off*, *up*, *down*, and *out*. Verb + particle combinations carry their own meanings. In other words, the verb and the particle work together to create meaning.

The plane **took off** ten minutes ago. ["left the ground"]

We **turned in** our papers. ["submitted"]

You can find the definitions of phrasal verbs in most dictionaries made for learners of English.

Phrasal verbs can appear in all the tense aspect combinations you have studied so far. The following chart includes the tense-aspect combinations for *turn up*:

	Present	Past	Future
Simple	turn/turns up	turned up	will turn up
Progressive	am/is/are turning up	was/were turning up	will be turning up
Perfect	has/have turned up	had turned up	will have turned up
Perfect Progressive	has/have been turning up	had been turning up	will have been turning up

exercise   19-1

Complete the following chart using the correct forms of the phrasal verb go out. *Remember that* go *is an irregular verb.*

	Present	Past	Future
Simple	_____	_____	_____
Progressive	_____	_____	_____
Perfect	_____	_____	_____
Perfect Progressive	_____	_____	_____

exercise   19-2

Complete each sentence with the form of the phrasal verb indicated in parentheses.

   EXAMPLE: They *took apart* (take apart, simple past) the engine.

1. The towing company _____ (take away, present perfect) the old car.

2. He _____ (put on, past progressive) his hat when the doorbell rang.

3. We _____ (find out, simple future) the results today.

4. I _____ (look up, present progressive) their phone number.

5. I _____ (sign up, future progressive) for four courses this term.

6. The planning committee _____ (put off, past perfect) the event once again.

7. Ray _____ (read through, future perfect) the report by Friday.

8. The publishing company _____ (put out, present perfect progressive) a new book every month.

9. By the end of the day, the actors _____ (go over, future perfect progressive) their lines for ten hours.

10. We _____ (take out, simple present) the trash every Thursday night.

11. The tour guide _____ (point out, simple past) some important sites.

12. For years, Lixing _____ (pay back, past perfect progressive) his loan month by month.

Phrasal Verbs in the Passive Voice

Phrasal verbs may also be used in the passive voice:

	Present	Past	Future
Simple	am/is/are picked up	was/were picked up	will be picked up
Progressive	am/is/are being picked up	was/were being picked up	NOT COMMON
Perfect	has/have been picked up	had been picked up	will have been picked up

exercise   19-3

Complete the following chart using the correct passive forms of the phrasal verb set up. *Remember that* set *is an irregular verb.*

	Present	Past	Future
Simple	_____	_____	_____
Progressive	_____	_____	NOT COMMON
Perfect	_____	_____	_____

exercise   19-4

Complete each sentence with the passive form of the phrasal verb indicated in parentheses.

EXAMPLE: The interviews *were written up* (write up, simple past) in time for the conference.

1. All the food at the party _____ (eat up, past perfect).

2. Our car _____ (block in, simple past) by another car.

3. The fire _____ (put out, present perfect).

4. His photograph _____ (blow up, simple future) and published in the local newspaper.

5. The project _____ (slow down, present progressive) by endless regulations.

6. Change _____ (bring about, simple present) only through much effort.

7. Their house _____ (break into, past progressive), so we called the police.

8. By next year, three new products _____ (bring out, future perfect).

Separable Phrasal Verbs

Phrasal verbs that take direct objects are often separable: the direct objects can be placed between the verb and the particle.

>   Angela **threw away** *the letter.*
>   Angela **threw** *the letter* **away**.

When the direct object is a pronoun, it must be placed between the verb and the particle.

>   Angela **threw** *it* **away**.

 **exercise   19-5**

Rewrite the following sentences so that the direct object is between the verb and the particle. Then rewrite the sentence replacing the direct object with a pronoun.

>   EXAMPLE: The instructor quickly passed out the exams.
>   *The instructor quickly passed the exams out.*
>   *The instructor quickly passed them out.*

1. She brought back the books yesterday.

    _____

    _____

2. They called off the game.

    _____

    _____

3. I checked out the book on Monday.

    _____

    _____

4. I crossed out some names.

    _____

    _____

5. Someone turned off the washing machine.

    _____

    _____

6. I called up my parents last night.

    _____

    _____

7. She closed up her suitcase and put it on the scale.

   _____

   _____

8. I cleaned out my desk this morning.

   _____

   _____

9. She wrote down the number.

   _____

   _____

10. They gave away their old furniture.

   _____

   _____

11. Victor helped out his sister.

   _____

   _____

12. She took down a map and gave it to us.

   _____

   _____

Forming Negatives

You studied the ways to make verbs negative in Parts I, II, and III. Phrasal verbs follow these same patterns.

Active Voice

TENSE/ASPECT	PRESENT	PAST	FUTURE
simple	does/do not turn out	did not turn out	will not turn out
progressive	am/is/are not turning out	was/were not turning out	will not be turning out
perfect	has/have not turned out	had not turned out	will not have turned out
perfect progressive	has/have not been turning out	had not been turning out	will not have been turning out

Passive Voice

TENSE/ASPECT	PRESENT	PAST	FUTURE
simple	am/is/are not picked up	was/were not picked up	will not be picked up
progressive	am/is/are not being picked up	was/were not being picked up	NOT COMMON
perfect	has/have not been picked up	had not been picked up	will not have been picked up

exercise   19-6

Make each of the following sentences negative.

EXAMPLE: The wind blew it down.
The wind did not blow it down.

1. Jacob is writing down the address.

   _____

2. She has booted up the computer.

   _____

3. The hot weather was wearing us down.

   _____

4. The books were brought back yesterday.

   _____

5. The painting on the sidewalk has been washed off.

   _____

6. I am bringing my friend over tonight.

   _____

7. They vote down most proposals.

   _____

8. He made up the story.

   _____

9. I will print out my paper on that printer.

   _____

10. The report was turned in on time.

    _____

11. She set it down carefully.

    _____

12. They had been locked out of their car before.

    _____

Modal Auxiliary Verbs

Modal auxiliary verbs appear before main verbs. They are used for a number of purposes. Here are some of the most common:

INDICATE ABILITY: She **can** speak English.

GIVE ADVICE: You **should** see a doctor.

EXPRESS CERTAINTY: We **will** finish by 8:00.

INDICATE POSSIBILITY: It **may** rain tonight.

INDICATE OBLIGATION: You **must** attend the last class.

GIVE PERMISSION: You **may** use your dictionaries during the exam.

INDICATE PAST HABIT: When I was little, we **would** go swimming every day.

Unlike other verbs, modal verbs have only one form. In other words, no -s is added to modal verbs to indicate third-person singular.

He/she/it **can/should/will/may/must** move.

exercise	20-1

Complete each sentence with the modal auxiliary verb that provides the meaning indicated in parentheses.

1. You _____ (certainty) receive a flight confirmation in the mail.

2. We _____ (advice) leave in ten minutes.

3. There _____ (possibility) be a storm tonight.

4. A notary public _____ (obligation) sign the form.

5. Alicia _____ (ability) draw well.

6. As a child, he _____ (past habit) play soccer every day.

7. _____ (permission) I borrow your pencil?

8. Pets _____ (obligation) be on leashes.

9. I _____ (possibility) leave work early tonight.

10. The package _____ (certainty) be delivered by noon.

11. They _____ (advice) be more careful.

12. _____ (ability) you come with us on Saturday?

13. You _____ (permission) enter the restricted area.

14. When we lived in San Diego, we _____ (past habit) often go to the beach.

Semi-Modal Auxiliary Verbs

English also has semi-modal auxiliary verbs. They are used for many of the same purposes as modal auxiliary verbs.

> INDICATE ABILITY: He **is able to** speak three different languages.
>
> GIVE ADVICE: You **ought to** finish the report.
>
> EXPRESS CERTAINTY: We **are going to** complete the project tonight.
>
> INDICATE OBLIGATION: You **have to** attend the meeting.
>
> INDICATE PAST HABIT: We **used to** play basketball together.

Unlike one-word modal verbs, most semi-modals are marked for number and tense.

> I **am** able to go.   I **was** able to go.
> You **have** to give a speech.   You **had** to give a speech.
> We **are** going to leave.   We **were** going to leave.
> They **have** to work late.   They **had** to work late.

Used to is an exception. It has only one form and always refers to the past. *Ought to* is another exception. It does not change form; however, the main verb that follows it can.

> It **ought to** be easy.   It **ought to** have been easy.

exercise   20-2

Complete each sentence with the semi-modal verb that provides the meaning indicated in parentheses. Use present tense forms.

1. You _____ (certainty) receive an award at the ceremony.

2. We _____ (advice) exercise daily.

3. Jorge and I _____ (past habit) play in a band.

4. We _____ (obligation) pay our tuition by Friday.

5. Devin _____ (ability) run the mile in five minutes.

6. I _____ (past habit) live in New York City.

7. He _____ (advice) take a multivitamin every morning.

8. You _____ (obligation) have a password.

9. They _____ (ability) help us move into our new apartment.

10. The concert _____ (certainty) start at 8:00.

 **exercise 20-3**

Complete each sentence with the semi-modal verb that provides the meaning indicated in parentheses. Use the past tense if possible.

1. It _____ (certainty) rain, so we left early.

2. She _____ (advice) have rested.

3. We _____ (obligation) pay a service charge.

4. The teacher _____ (ability) remember everyone's name.

5. I _____ (certainty) go with them, but then I got sick.

6. My father _____ (advice) have had a checkup yesterday.

7. Amber _____ (obligation) retype her paper, because she lost her disk.

8. They _____ (ability) hike long distances when they were young.

Combining Semi-Modals

Sometimes semi-modals can be used with other semi-modals or after some regular modals.

> They **are going to have to** finish their papers by Friday. [semi-modal + semi-modal]
> I **will have to** call you back later. [modal + semi-modal]

Underline the modals and circle the semi-modals in the following sentences.

1. I might be able to help you on Thursday.

2. They are going to be able to take a vacation next month.

3. She might have to quit her job.

4. You are going to have to work hard.

5. We will have to take notes at the lecture.

Forming Negatives

To make a modal negative, place *not* after it.

> I should **not** eat so much at lunch.

Write the combination of *can* and *not* as one word: *cannot.* Write the other combinations as two words.

To make a semi-modal containing the verb *be* negative, place *not* directly after the *be* verb.

> Our teacher is **not** going to cancel the exam.

To make a semi-modal containing the verb *have* negative, place the auxiliary verb *do* and *not* before it.

> Jay **does not** have to go to class today.

exercise   20-5

Complete each of the following sentences using a negative form of the modal or semi-modal provided.

> EXAMPLE: We, be going to
> *We are not going to* go to the movies tonight.

1. You, should

   _____ smoke in this restaurant.

2. We, can

   _____ escape the heat today.

3. Martin, be able to

_____ find his books.

4. The supervisor, be going to

_____ be happy.

5. They, may

_____ stay very long.

6. You, must

_____ tell anyone.

7. We, would

When we were little, _____ go inside until 10:00.

8. They, will

For some reason, _____ answer their phone.

9. I, have to

Tomorrow, _____ get up early.

10. You, should

_____ worry so much.

Forming Contractions

Contractions are commonly used in conversation and informal writing.

are + not = aren't	is + not = isn't
do + not = don't	does + not = doesn't
cannot = can't	should + not = shouldn't
will + not = won't	must + not = mustn't

May not is never contracted.

exercise	**20-6**

Rewrite the sentences in exercise 20-5 using contractions. If may not *appears, leave the line blank.*

1. _____

2. _____

3. _____

4. _____

5. _____

6. _____

7. _____

8. _____

9. _____

10. _____

Modal Perfect Verbs

Modal perfect verbs follow these patterns:

ACTIVE VOICE: modal + *have* + perfect/passive form of the verb

PASSIVE VOICE: modal + *have been* + perfect/passive form of the verb

These are some of the common uses:

EXPRESSION OF REGRET: **I should have** tried harder.

CRITICISM OF A PAST ACTION OR LACK OF ACTION: He **should have** told me. She **could have** at least called. They **ought to have** told me.

EXPRESSION OF AN EXPECTATION ABOUT AN EVENT THAT MAY NOT HAVE HAPPENED: They **should have** arrived by now.

GUESS ABOUT A PAST EVENT: The window **may have been** shattered by the wind. I **might have** met him before.

STRONG CONJECTURE ABOUT A PAST EVENT: Someone **must have** stolen my purse.

exercise	20-7

Complete each sentence with the modal perfect verb that provides the meaning indicated in parentheses.

1. I ＿＿＿＿＿＿ (regret, active voice) sent her a birthday card.

2. We ＿＿＿＿＿＿ (expectation, active voice) heard from them by now.

3. They ＿＿＿＿＿＿ (criticism, active voice) invited everyone in class, not just a few people.

4. The store ＿＿＿＿＿＿ (guess, passive voice) closed early because of an emergency.

5. The Angels ＿＿＿＿＿＿ (strong conjecture, active voice) won.

6. By this time, everyone ＿＿＿＿＿＿ (expectation, active voice) been ready.

7. You ＿＿＿＿＿＿ (guess, active voice) lost your wallet in the café.

8. I ＿＿＿＿＿＿ (regret, active voice) brought an umbrella.

9. There ＿＿＿＿＿＿ (strong conjecture, active voice) been an accident in this intersection.

10. The package ＿＿＿＿＿＿ (criticism, passive voice) delivered earlier.

PART VI

GERUND AND INFINITIVE COMPLEMENTS

Gerunds and infinitives are verb forms, but they are not used as the main verbs in sentences. Gerunds are formed by adding *-ing* to the base form of a verb: *running, talking, doing.* (The *-ing* form is often called the *present participle.*) Infinitives consist of two parts: the infinitive marker *to* and the base form of a verb: *to run, to talk, to do.* Gerunds and infinitives can follow main verbs.

She enjoys **playing** the guitar.

He promised **to sing** for us.

Some verbs, such as *enjoy*, are followed by gerunds. Others, such as *promise*, are followed by infinitives. But some verbs can be followed by either gerunds or infinitives.

I like **reading** mysteries.

I like **to read** mysteries.

Generally, gerunds signal that an action has happened or is especially vivid. Infinitives indicate future or hypothetical events.

Gerunds

Gerunds have four forms:

SIMPLE: She avoids **driving** during rush hour.

PERFECT: He admits **having taken** the documents.

PASSIVE: They dislike always **being put** in the last row.

PASSIVE PERFECT: I appreciate **having been given** this opportunity.

The following verbs can be followed by gerunds but cannot be followed by infinitives:

admit	appreciate	avoid	consider
delay	deny	dislike	enjoy
finish	keep	mind	miss
quit	recommend	risk	suggest

exercise 21-1

Complete each sentence with the form of the gerund indicated in parentheses.

> EXAMPLE: Albert considered *living* (live, simple) abroad for a year.

1. My brother and his wife delayed _____ (have, simple) children until they were settled.

2. I miss _____ (surprise, passive) on my birthday by my grandfather.

3. The politician denied _____ (mention, perfect) a possible tax increase.

4. I keep _____ (try, simple) his number, but he doesn't answer.

5. They didn't mind _____ (invite, passive perfect) at the last minute.

6. The doctor recommended _____ (eat, simple) more fruits and vegetables.

7. I appreciate _____ (choose, passive perfect) as your representative.

8. The committee finished _____ (review, simple) the applications yesterday.

9. We admitted _____ (be, perfect) the source of the trouble.

10. He dislikes _____ (treat, passive) as a child.

11. The tour guide suggested _____ (stop, simple) for lunch at this restaurant.

12. Fortunately, we avoided _____ (give, passive) a ticket.

13. For some reason, she quit _____ (play, simple) the piano a year ago.

14. When he made the repair, he risked _____ (damage, simple) the whole system.

15. We enjoyed _____ (introduce, passive) to your family.

exercise   21-2

Use gerunds to answer the following questions.

> EXAMPLE: What sport do you like playing?
> *I like playing soccer.*

1. What do you enjoying doing on holidays?

   _____

2. What have you avoided doing in the past year?

   _____

3. What do you dislike doing on the weekend?

   _____

4. What story did you like being told when you were a child?

   _____

5. Whom do you miss seeing whom you cannot see now?

   _____

Infinitives

Infinitives have a number of forms. These are the most common:

SIMPLE: Eva wants **to become** a lawyer.

PROGRESSIVE: They seem **to be telling** the truth.

PERFECT: He hopes **to have finished** his work by next Friday.

PASSIVE: Anna deserves **to be promoted**.

PASSIVE PERFECT: We pretended **to have been surprised**.

The following verbs can be followed by infinitives but cannot be followed by gerunds:

agree	choose	decide	deserve
expect	fail	hope	intend
manage	need	offer	plan
pretend	promise	seem	want

exercise   **22-1**

Complete each sentence with the form of the infinitive indicated in parentheses.

> EXAMPLE: Janine managed *to find* (find, simple) an apartment on the first day of her search.

1. I plan _____ (work, progressive) full-time next year.

2. He agreed _____ (pay, simple) me for the photographs.

3. She hopes _____ (earn, perfect) a raise by the end of this year.

4. The child pretended _____ (faint, perfect).

5. Shoba deserves _____ (hire, passive) for the new position.

6. Everyone offered _____ (help, simple) us.

7. The announcement seems _____ (leak, passive perfect) to the press.

8. In order to get that job, he needs _____ (network, progressive).

9. The director expected _____ (receive, perfect) the report by now.

10. The reporter had wanted _____ (give, passive) a different assignment.

11. I promise _____ (meet, simple) you there at 5:00.

12. My parents decided _____ (stay, simple) an extra week.

13. He failed _____ (turn in, simple) the work on time.

14. Our neighbors intend _____ (move, simple) next year.

15. The company chose _____ (close, simple) one of the plants.

---

exercise | **22-2**

Use infinitives to answer the following questions.

> EXAMPLE: What did you expect to learn in this book?
> *I expected to learn about English verbs.*

1. Where do you plan to go this weekend?

_____

2. Where do you intend to be next year at this time?

_____

3. What do you need to buy this week?

_____

4. What do you want to have for dinner?

_____

5. What do you expect to study next term?

_____

Verbs Followed by a Noun Phrase and an Infinitive

Some verbs are followed by both a noun phrase (a pronoun or a noun and any of its modifiers) and an infinitive:

advise	allow	cause	encourage
invite	order	permit	persuade
require	teach	tell	urge

 **exercise**   **22-3**

Complete each of the following sentences using the noun phrase provided and the simple form of the infinitive.

> EXAMPLE: us, go
> The teacher encouraged *us to go* to the lecture.

1. him, exercise

   Dr. Olson advised _____ more frequently.

2. us, attend

   Carl invited _____ his piano recital.

3. my sister, ride

   My brother taught _____ a bike.

4. me, turn

   He told _____ left at the corner.

5. people, touch

   The museum guide permitted _____ some of the exhibits.

6. Brent and me, be

   The accident caused _____ more careful the next time.

7. local artists, hang

   Laura Adams allowed _____ their paintings in her restaurant.

8. the protesters, leave

   The police ordered _____.

9. me, rethink

   My parents persuaded _____ my plan.

10. employers, provide

    The new law required _____ safety training.

11. Robyn, major

    Mr. Pruett encouraged _____ in biology.

12. everyone, conserve

    The president urged _____ energy.

Gerunds or Infinitives

Some verbs can be followed by either gerunds or infinitives. Sometimes there is no significant difference in meaning between a sentence with a gerund and a sentence with an infinitive.

He began **humming**.

He began **to hum**.

The most common verbs falling into this category are the following three verbs dealing with time:

begin　　　　　　continue　　　　　　start

The verb *stop*, however, is used to express two different meanings.

We stopped singing. [The singing has ended.]

We stopped to sing. [The singing has not started yet.]

After verbs dealing with emotion, the gerund is generally used to express the vividness of an action, an event, or a state or to indicate its actual occurrence. The infinitive usually indicates a future, potential, or hypothetical action, event, or state.

I usually prefer **cooking** my own food, but tonight I would prefer **to go** out.

The following verbs fall into this category:

hate　　　　like　　　　　love　　　　　prefer

Some verbs dealing with memory signal different time sequences, depending on whether a gerund or an infinitive is used.

I remember **locking** the door. [The door was locked; then the action of locking was remembered.]

I remembered **to lock** the door. [The remembering of a responsibility took place before the action of locking was performed.]

The following verbs fall into this category:

remember　　　　　forget　　　　　　regret

exercise   23-1

Underline the gerund or infinitive. Circle the reason that the gerund or the infinitive is used. If either a gerund or infinitive could be used, circle "No significant change in meaning."

1. It started to rain.

   Memory of action   **Vivid depiction**   **No significant change in meaning**

2. I remembered to bring a lunch.

   Memory to perform action   **Vivid depiction**   **No significant change in meaning**

3. He regretted quitting that job.

   Memory of action   **Memory to perform action**   **Vivid depiction**

4. They continued to talk during the entire movie.

   Actual occurrence   **Vivid depiction**   **No significant change in meaning**

5. My friends and I love going to the beach.

   Memory of action   **Vivid depiction**   **No significant change in meaning**

6. I would hate to clean up that mess.

   Actual occurrence   **Hypothetical occurrence**   **Vivid depiction**

7. Laxmi remembers returning the books to the library.

   Memory of action   **Memory to perform action**   **Vivid depiction**

8. My neighbors like throwing huge parties.

   Actual occurrence   **Vivid depiction**   **Potential occurrence**

9. The car began to make strange noises.

   Actual occurrence   **Vivid depiction**   **No significant change in meaning**

10. I prefer to take classes at night.

    Vivid depiction   **Potential occurrence**   **No significant change in meaning**

Chart of Irregular Verbs

Base Form	-s Form (Present Tense, Third Person, Singular)	-ing Form (Present Participle)	Past Form	-en Form (Past Participle)
be	is (third-person singular) am (first-person singular) are (other person/ number combinations)	being	was (first- and third-person singular) were (other person/number combinations)	been
become	becomes	becoming	became	become
begin	begins	beginning	began	begun
blow	blows	blowing	blew	blown
break	breaks	breaking	broke	broken
bring	brings	bringing	brought	brought
broadcast	broadcasts	broadcasting	broadcasted, broadcast	broadcasted, broadcast
build	builds	building	built	built
buy	buys	buying	bought	bought
choose	chooses	choosing	chose	chosen

Base Form	-s Form (Present Tense, Third Person, Singular)	-ing Form (Present Participle)	Past Form	-en Form (Past Participle)
come	comes	coming	came	come
cost	costs	costing	cost	cost
cut	cuts	cutting	cut	cut
do	does	doing	did	done
dream	dreams	dreaming	dreamed, dreamt	dreamed, dreamt
drink	drinks	drinking	drank	drunk
drive	drives	driving	drove	driven
eat	eats	eating	ate	eaten
fall	falls	falling	fell	fallen
feel	feels	feeling	felt	felt
find	finds	finding	found	found
fly	flies	flying	flew	flown
forget	forgets	forgetting	forgot	forgotten
get	gets	getting	got	gotten, got
give	gives	giving	gave	given
go	goes	going	went	gone
grow	grows	growing	grew	grown
hang (suspend)	hangs	hanging	hung	hung

Base Form	-*s* Form (Present Tense, Third Person, Singular)	-*ing* Form (Present Participle)	Past Form	-*en* Form (Past Participle)
have	has	having	had	had
hear	hears	hearing	heard	heard
hit	hits	hitting	hit	hit
hold	holds	holding	held	held
hurt	hurts	hurting	hurt	hurt
keep	keeps	keeping	kept	kept
know	knows	knowing	knew	known
lead	leads	leading	led	led
leave	leaves	leaving	left	left
lend	lends	lending	lent	lent
let	lets	letting	let	let
lie (to rest or recline)	lies	lying	lay	lain
lose	loses	losing	lost	lost
make	makes	making	made	made
meet	meets	meeting	met	met
pay	pays	paying	paid	paid
put	puts	putting	put	put
quit	quits	quitting	quit	quit

Base Form	-s Form (Present Tense, Third Person, Singular)	-ing Form (Present Participle)	Past Form	-en Form (Past Participle)
read	reads	reading	read	read
ride	rides	riding	rode	ridden
ring	rings	ringing	rang	rung
rise	rises	rising	rose	risen
run	runs	running	ran	run
say	says	saying	said	said
see	sees	seeing	saw	seen
sell	sells	selling	sold	sold
send	sends	sending	sent	sent
set	sets	setting	set	set
shake	shakes	shaking	shook	shaken
show	shows	showing	showed	showed, shown
sing	sings	singing	sang	sung
sink	sinks	sinking	sank	sunk
sit	sits	sitting	sat	sat
sleep	sleeps	sleeping	slept	slept
speak	speaks	speaking	spoke	spoken
spend	spends	spending	spent	spent

Base Form	-s Form (Present Tense, Third Person, Singular)	-ing Form (Present Participle)	Past Form	-en Form (Past Participle)
spread	spreads	spreading	spread	spread
stand	stands	standing	stood	stood
steal	steals	stealing	stole	stolen
take	takes	taking	took	taken
teach	teaches	teaching	taught	taught
tell	tells	telling	told	told
think	thinks	thinking	thought	thought
throw	throws	throwing	threw	thrown
understand	understands	understanding	understood	understood
wear	wears	wearing	wore	worn
win	wins	winning	won	won
write	writes	writing	wrote	written

Glossary

ASPECT   A grammatical category that provides information about the duration or completeness of an action, a state, or an event. Aspect may also provide information about actions, states, or events in relation to a specific time or to another action, state, or event.

AUXILIARY VERB   A specialized verb that provides information about tense, aspect, or modality. *Be, have*, and *do* can be used as auxiliary verbs, although they can also be used as main verbs. Words such as *must, can*, and *may* are modal auxiliary verbs. Modal auxiliary verbs are used to signal obligation, ability, possibility, and other meanings.

GERUND   The *-ing* form of a verb, functioning as a noun. Some verbs can be followed by gerunds (e.g., I enjoy **going** to concerts.).

HYPOTHETICAL CONDITIONAL   A grammatical structure consisting of two parts: an *if* clause that expresses an impossible or only slightly possible occurrence and a consequence clause, sometimes introduced by *then.*

IMPERATIVE   A grammatical structure characterized by the presence of the base form of a verb and the absence of a subject. The subject *you* is usually not expressed (e.g., Be quiet.). Imperatives are generally used in instructions, directions, warnings, and commands.

INFINITIVE   The base form of a verb preceded by *to*. When an infinitive follows a verb, it functions as a noun (e.g., We want **to see** you soon.).

PHRASAL VERB   A verb + particle combination that carries a specific meaning (e.g., **Turn in** your paper.).

PRONOUN   Usually a single word, such as *it, she,* or *I*, which functions as a noun phrase. A pronoun is marked for person (first, second, or third) and number (singular or plural).

SUBJECT (SINGULAR, PLURAL, NONCOUNT)   The noun phrase (sometimes just a single noun or a pronoun) that carries out the action or assumes the state expressed by the verb. Singular subjects refer to one entity; plural subjects refer to more than one entity. Noncount subjects are not able to be counted (e.g., furniture, sugar). A verb conjugated as third person singular is used with a noncount noun.

TENSE   A grammatical category that provides information about the placement in time of an action, a state, or an event.

VOICE (ACTIVE AND PASSIVE)   The grammatical category that provides information about the way a subject is related to a verb. In the active voice, the subject generally performs an action, whereas in the passive voice, the subject generally undergoes the action.

WH-QUESTIONS   Questions that elicit specific pieces of information and that are introduced by question words usually beginning with the letters *w* and *h* (e.g., *who, what, where, why*). The question word *how* is an exception.

YES/NO QUESTIONS   Questions that can be answered "yes" or "no," although other responses such as "maybe" are possible.

Answer Key

Part I The Present Tense
Unit 1 Simple Present

1-1

1.	eat	habitual action
2.	carries	habitual action
3.	speak	fact
4.	produces	fact
5.	make	custom
6.	watches	habitual action
7.	says	custom
8.	begins	future time
9.	live	fact
10.	grow	fact
11.	wear	custom
12.	shake, meet	custom

1-2

The correct subjects and verbs are provided. Other parts of the sentence may vary.
1. She always **makes** strawberry pies for the Fourth of July.
2. I **take** the garbage out every Tuesday night.
3. It **gives** me a headache.
4. They **come** to our house on Labor Day.
5. I **use** my computer every day.
6. He **leaves** in ten minutes.
7. They **like** the theater.
8. She **writes** poetry and short stories.
9. We **listen** to the baseball games on KXLE.
10. It **contains** something fragile.
11. It **starts** at 9:00.
12. He **understands** the theory.

1-3

1. He **does not go** to school every day.
2. My roommate **does not like** snakes.
3. You **do not know** my family.
4. The owner **does not open** the store every day at 8:00.
5. We **do not help** our neighbors.
6. My friends **do not send** me letters.
7. I **do not feel** tired.
8. She **does not speak** five different languages.
9. They **do not study** in the library.
10. We **do not listen** to pop music.
11. They **do not grow** tomatoes in their backyard.
12. This car **does not run** well.

1-4

1. He **doesn't go** to school every day.
2. My roommate **doesn't like** snakes.
3. You **don't know** my family.
4. The owner **doesn't open** the store every day at 8:00.

5. We **don't help** our neighbors.
6. My friends **don't send** me letters.
7. I **don't feel** tired.
8. She **doesn't speak** five different languages.
9. They **don't study** in the library.
10. We **don't listen** to pop music.
11. They **don't grow** tomatoes in their backyard.
12. This car **doesn't run** well.

1-5
1. **Does** the artist **show** his work at a local gallery?
2. **Do** they **meet** on Thursday mornings?
3. **Does** she **work** hard?
4. **Do** you **commute** to work?
5. **Does** it **seem** like a good decision?
6. **Does** this **work** require patience?
7. **Do** the Carsons **live** in a small town?
8. **Don't** you **believe** my story?
9. **Does** the patient **feel** better?
10. **Does** the lecture **end** at 5:30?
11. **Does** the plot **involve** many characters?
12. **Do** most students **complete** the program in four years?

1-6
1. Who **knows** the answer?
2. How **does** she **look**?
3. Why **do** they always **go** to that restaurant?
4. How often **do** they **go** golfing?
5. Where **do** we **turn** left?
6. How much **does** the notebook **cost**?
7. Who **worries** too much?
8. How often **do** you **exercise** at the gym?
9. What **do** Jerry and Carol **repair**?
10. What **does** she **teach**?
11. Whom **does** Mark **blame** for his problems?
12. Where **do** many people **go** for their vacations?

Unit 2 *Be* Verb Forms

2-1
1. am
2. are, am
3. are
4. is
5. is
6. are
7. are
8. am
9. is
10. is
11. is
12. are

2-2
1. is
2. are
3. are
4. is
5. are
6. is

7. is
8. are
9. are
10. is
11. is
12. is

2-3

1. **She's** a student.
2. **I'm** an engineer.
3. **There's** a test on Tuesday.
4. **You're** next.
5. **It's** difficult.
6. **We're** from Canada.
7. **He's** a supervisor.
8. **They're** really funny.
9. **I'm** sick today.
10. **There's** a package for you on the table.
11. **He's** first on the list.
12. **It's** cold in here.

2-4

1. **She's not** a student.
2. **I'm not** an engineer.
3. **There's not** a test on Tuesday.
4. **You're not** next.
5. **It's not** difficult.
6. **We're not** from Canada.
7. **He's not** a supervisor.
8. **They're not** really funny.
9. **I'm not** sick today.
10. **There's not** a package for you on the table.
11. **He's not** first on the list.
12. **It's not** cold in here.

2-5

1. isn't
2. aren't
3. isn't
4. aren't
5. aren't
6. isn't

2-6

1. **Is** Portland in the state of Oregon?
2. **Is** your car in the garage?
3. **Is** he in a good mood?
4. **Are** they friends?
5. **Is** Sam depressed?
6. **Is** her computer broken?
7. **Are** there many items on the menu?
8. **Is** the coffee too hot?
9. **Is** the city hall the oldest building in town?
10. **Is** there a bank near here?
11. **Is** the museum open on Thursday evenings?
12. **Are** the lights off?

2-7

1. Who **is** the editor of the local newspaper?
2. How tall **is** she?
3. Who **are** they?

4. Where **is** his roommate right now?
5. When **is** the graduation ceremony?
6. What color **is** the house?
7. What **is** that?
8. Where **are** the scissors?
9. Who **is** the producer?
10. Where **are** the children?
11. How late **is** the library open?
12. Where **are** they?

Unit 3 Present Progressive (*Be* Verb + *-ing*)

3-1

1. am studying	temporary situation
2. are going	future time
3. am writing	activity in progress
4. is pulling	activity in progress
5. are moving	future time
6. are acting	activity in progress
7. am using	temporary situation
8. are eating	future time (or activity in progress if said while eating)
9. is having	temporary situation
10. is mowing	activity in progress
11. am turning	future time
12. is living	temporary situation
13. is snowing	activity in progress
14. are standing	activity in progress
15. are speaking	activity in progress
16. is growing	activity in progress

3-2

1. sells
2. is selling
3. am boiling
4. boils
5. visit
6. are visiting
7. goes
8. is going
9. am doing
10. do

3-3

The correct subjects and verbs are provided. Other parts of the sentence may vary.
1. **He's paying** for dinner.
2. **It's hailing**.
3. **We're meeting** in the conference room.
4. Right now **they're losing** the game.
5. **She's waiting** in line.
6. **You're carrying** a heavy backpack.
7. **I'm wearing** a hat today.
8. **We're reading** the same book.
9. **She's calling** the movie theater.
10. **He's selling** his old bicycle.
11. **They're staying** at home tonight.
12. **I'm assisting** a customer right now.

3-4

1. I **am not buying** a new car tomorrow.
2. She **is not studying**.
3. We **are not leaving** soon.
4. They **are not coming** with us.
5. Carla **is not living** with her parents.
6. I **am not cooking** dinner tonight.
7. The band **is not performing** tonight.
8. My mother **is not visiting** this weekend.
9. They **are not sleeping**.
10. We **are not going** to the park today.
11. They **are not fixing** the road.
12. She **is not quitting** her job.

3-5

1. **I'm not buying** a new car tomorrow.
2. **She's not studying**. OR She **isn't studying**.
3. **We're not leaving** soon. OR We **aren't leaving** soon.
4. **They're not coming** with us. OR They **aren't coming** with us.
5. **Carla's not living** with her parents. OR Carla **isn't living** with her parents.
6. **I'm not cooking** dinner tonight.
7. The **band's not performing** tonight. OR The band **isn't performing** tonight.
8. My **mother's not visiting** this weekend. OR My mother **isn't visiting** this weekend.
9. **They're not sleeping**. OR They **aren't sleeping**.
10. **We're not going** to the park today. OR We **aren't going** to the park today.
11. **They're not fixing** the road. OR They **aren't fixing** the road.
12. **She's not quitting** her job. OR She **isn't quitting** her job.

3-6

1. **Is** the mail carrier **delivering** a package to our house?
2. **Is** the boat **sinking**?
3. **Are** they **causing** trouble?
4. **Is** he **worrying** about his course grade?
5. **Is** Helen **publishing** her autobiography?
6. **Is** the teacher **inviting** everyone in class to a party?
7. **Is** the committee **announcing** the winner of the contest today?
8. **Is** the engineer **explaining** the process?
9. **Is** Mandy **singing** at her sister's wedding?
10. **Is** the company **expanding**?
11. **Is** Phil **arranging** the conference?
12. **Are** the police **accusing** him of the crime?

3-7

1. What **are** they **eating**?
2. Who **is coming** along?
3. What **are** we **watching** on television tonight?
4. What **is** she **showing** them?
5. Whom **are** you **meeting**?
6. Why **are** they **wearing** special clothes?
7. What **is** he **hoping** for?
8. What **is happening**?
9. What **are** Alex and Terry **playing**?
10. Where **are** they **moving**?
11. Who **is staring** at us?
12. Who **is winning**?

Unit 4 Present Perfect

4-1

1. have built
2. have eaten
3. have lent
4. have spoken
5. has fallen
6. have known
7. have sold
8. has rained
9. have kept
10. has spent
11. have cut

4-2

1. He's rented
2. It's worked
3. We've been
4. They've lost
5. She's waited
6. You've reached
7. I've applied
8. We've developed
9. She's ignored
10. He's found
11. They've gone
12. I've forgotten

4-3

1. They **have not chosen** a location for the conference.
2. She **has not completed** her work.
3. We **have not studied** our options.
4. I **have not received** my test results.
5. You **have not mentioned** his name before.
6. He **has not reviewed** the plans.
7. It **has not disappeared**.

4-4

1. They **haven't chosen** a location for the conference.
2. She **hasn't completed** her work.
3. We **haven't studied** our options.
4. I **haven't received** my test results.
5. You **haven't mentioned** his name before.
6. He **hasn't reviewed** the plans.
7. It **hasn't disappeared**.

4-5

1. **Have** you **put** the dishes away?
2. **Have** they **offered** her a new job?
3. **Have** we **received** good news?
4. **Has** he **checked** the oil in the car?
5. **Has** Jackson **obtained** a driver's license?
6. **Has** the new student **arrived**?
7. **Has** Jeanette **responded** to our message?
8. **Have** the archaeologists **discovered** new fossils?
9. **Have** you **made** your lunch?
10. **Has** the business **expanded**?
11. **Has** Sarah **arranged** the meeting?
12. **Has** the program **been** successful?

4-6

1. What **have** they **given** to charities?
2. Who **has appeared** on television?
3. How many games **has** she **missed**?
4. Who **has passed** the first part of the test?
5. How many of his novels **have** you **read**?
6. What color **has** Les **painted** his house?
7. Who **has sung** at the White House?
8. What **has happened**?
9. Who **has influenced** your decision?
10. Which courses **has** he **taken**?
11. How many years **have** you **taught** English?
12. Whom **have** they **invited** to the party?

Unit 5 Present Perfect Progressive

5-1

1. has been hurting
2. has been causing
3. has been exercising
4. have been drinking
5. has been worrying
6. has been earning
7. have been paying
8. have been following
9. have been sitting
10. have been applying
11. have been helping
12. have been rising

5-2

1. He's been expecting
2. It's been changing
3. We've been developing
4. They've been checking
5. She's been exploring
6. You've been complaining
7. I've been calculating

5-3

1. He has not been ignoring
2. It has not been improving
3. We have not been commuting
4. They have not been buying
5. She has not been doing
6. You have not been finishing
7. I have not been riding

5-4

1. He hasn't been ignoring the evidence.
2. It hasn't been improving much.
3. We haven't been commuting together this year.
4. They haven't been buying much lately.
5. She hasn't been doing her work.
6. You haven't been finishing your projects on time.
7. I haven't been riding the bus to school.

5-5

1. **Have** you **been paying** all your bills on time?
2. **Has** the noise **been bothering** them?
3. **Has** traffic **been moving** slowly?

4. **Has** she **been waiting** a long time?
5. **Have** they **been reducing** the number of accidents?
6. **Has** the suspect **been lying**?
7. **Have** you **been reading** an interesting novel?
8. **Has** the government **been allowing** journalists into the country?
9. **Has** she **been keeping** good records?
10. **Have** they **been considering** the proposal?
11. **Has** he **been staying** close to home?
12. **Has** she **been making** progress?

5-6

1. Where **has** Paula **been traveling**?
2. How long **has** he **been living** in Miami?
3. What **have** they **been searching** for?
4. Who **has been watching** the children?
5. How often **have** they **been going** to the Virgin Islands?
6. What **has** the guide **been arranging**?
7. Who **has been taking** notes?
8. How long **have** you **been attending** the university?
9. What **have** they **been planning**?
10. What **has** he **been talking** about?
11. How **have** you **been feeling** lately?
12. How long **has** she **been standing** there?

Part II The Past Tense
Unit 6 Simple Past

6-1

1. worked
2. waited
3. remembered
4. needed
5. missed
6. sold
7. went
8. met
9. cut
10. wore

6-2

1. lived
2. have lived
3. have studied
4. studied
5. traveled
6. have traveled
7. have worked
8. worked
9. has built
10. built

6-3

1. He **did not come** to work on time.
2. My roommate **did not like** the movie.
3. She **did not understand** the problem.
4. We **did not take** a wrong turn.
5. The students **did not need** help with the homework.
6. The driver **did not blame** me for the accident.
7. I **did not listen** to the directions.
8. She **did not earn** a degree in economics.

9. He **did not calculate** the taxes.
10. They **did not complain** about the weather.

6-4

1. He **didn't come** to work on time.
2. My roommate **didn't like** the movie.
3. She **didn't understand** the problem.
4. We **didn't take** a wrong turn.
5. The students **didn't need** help with the homework.
6. The driver **didn't blame** me for the accident.
7. I **didn't listen** to the directions.
8. She **didn't earn** a degree in economics.
9. He **didn't calculate** the taxes.
10. They **didn't complain** about the weather.

6-5

1. **Did** they **elect** a new president?
2. **Did** she **deliver** the report?
3. **Did** you **expect** us earlier?
4. **Did** Tho **pass** his driver's test?
5. **Did** the committee **explore** the issues?
6. **Did** he **explain** the problem?
7. **Did** the director **have** an appointment at 3:00?
8. **Did** you **forget** the map?
9. **Did** the bank **lend** him some money?
10. **Did** they **offer** him a job?

6-6

1. Who **wrote** *Beloved*?
2. Who **won** the contest?
3. Which way **did** he **turn**?
4. How many countries **did** they **travel** to?
5. How long **did** you **teach** biology?
6. How much **did** the repair **cost**?
7. How long **did** they **stay** at the party?
8. How far **did** she **run**?
9. Where **did** they **move**?
10. How far **did** they **climb**?

Unit 7 *Be* Verb Forms

7-1

1. was
2. were
3. were
4. was
5. was
6. were
7. was
8. were
9. was
10. was

7-2

1. was
2. were
3. was
4. was
5. were
6. were

7. was
8. was
9. were
10. was

7-3

1. weren't
2. wasn't
3. weren't
4. wasn't
5. weren't
6. wasn't
7. weren't
8. weren't
9. weren't
10. wasn't

7-4

1. **Was** the concert in the park?
2. **Was** the road under construction?
3. **Was** everyone on time?
4. **Were** the textbooks expensive?
5. **Was** the job stressful?
6. **Was** the program a success?
7. **Were** there many apartments for rent?
8. **Was** the parking lot full?
9. **Were** the tickets free?
10. **Was** the computer on?

7-5

1. Who **was** the president of the United States in 1980?
2. How **was** the trip?
3. Where **were** his grandparents from?
4. Where **were** they?
5. When **was** the field trip?
6. How long **was** the gym open on Sunday?
7. What items **were** on sale?
8. How **was** the traffic?
9. Who **was** there?
10. How long **was** the movie?

Unit 8 Past Progressive (*Be* Verb + *-ing*)

8-1

1. was being
2. was ringing
3. was waiting, was dreaming
4. were living
5. was taking, was studying
6. was putting
7. was knocking, was getting
8. was raining
9. were going
10. were cleaning

8-2

1. complete action
2. action in progress
3. action in progress
4. complete action

5. action in progress
6. complete action
7. complete action
8. action in progress
9. action in progress
10. complete action

8-3

1. He **was not attending** a conference.
2. They **were not laughing**.
3. I **was not complaining** about the work.
4. She **was not helping** us.
5. Ted **was not studying** last night.
6. They **were not paying** attention.
7. I **was not talking** to myself.
8. You **were not speaking** loud enough.
9. They **were not doing** their homework.
10. We **were not trying** hard.

8-4

1. He **wasn't attending** a conference.
2. They **weren't laughing**.
3. I **wasn't complaining** about the work.
4. She **wasn't helping** us.
5. Ted **wasn't studying** last night.
6. They **weren't paying** attention.
7. I **wasn't talking** to myself.
8. You **weren't speaking** loud enough.
9. They **weren't doing** their homework.
10. We **weren't trying** hard.

8-5

1. **Was** the band **giving** a free concert?
2. **Was** the light **blinking** on and off?
3. **Were** you **watching** the championship on television?
4. **Were** they **being** careful?
5. **Was** it **snowing** all day?
6. **Were** Gabe and Don **singing** together?
7. **Were** they **closing** the store?
8. **Were** the companies **considering** a merger?
9. **Were** they **recycling** most of the waste products?
10. As young children, **were** they always **getting** into trouble?

8-6

1. Where **were** they **protesting**?
2. Who **was using** this computer?
3. What **were** you **watching** on television last night?
4. What **was** the committee **discussing**?
5. What **was bothering** them?
6. Who **was spreading** rumors?
7. Where **was** he **working**?
8. How fast **was** she **driving**?
9. What **was** he **reading** during class today?
10. Where **were** they **standing**?

Unit 9 Past Perfect

9-1

1. had attended
2. had held
3. had sold
4. had met
5. had felt
6. had hit
7. had sat
8. had run
9. had snowed
10. had been

9-2

1. arrived, had left
2. had finished, went
3. had assigned, completed
4. was, had worked
5. wore, had given
6. revised, had written
7. had knocked, entered
8. knew, had taken
9. read, had received
10. celebrated, had passed

9-3

1. They **had not met**
2. it **had not changed**
3. We **had not considered**
4. He **had not wanted**
5. She **had not driven**
6. You **had not spoken**
7. I **had not sent**

9-4

1. **They'd met** before.
   They **hadn't met** before.
2. Because **it'd changed** color, no one could see it.
   Because it **hadn't changed** color, no one could see it.
3. **We'd considered** all the possibilities.
   We **hadn't considered** all the possibilities.
4. **He'd wanted** help from us.
   He **hadn't wanted** help from us.
5. **She'd driven** to the party.
   She **hadn't driven** to the party.
6. **You'd spoken** English before you came to the United States.
   You **hadn't spoken** English before you came to the United States.
7. **I'd sent** my application in on time.
   I **hadn't sent** my application in on time.

9-5

1. **Hadn't** she **called** before she arrived?
2. **Hadn't** they **obtained** permission before they started the experiment?
3. **Had** Pat **won** the first race before he ran the second race?
4. **Had** they **closed** the road?
5. **Had** they **canceled** the game without prior notice?

1. Who **had received** job offers before they graduated?
2. How many track records **had** Peter **broken** by the age of eighteen?
3. How long **had** she **taught** English before she went to law school?
4. When **had** he **arrived** at the gate?
5. How long **had** they **dated** before they got married?

Unit 10 Past Perfect Progressive

1. had been working
2. had been discussing
3. had been studying
4. had been increasing
5. had been playing
6. had been raining
7. had been watching
8. had been writing
9. had been studying
10. had been working

10-2

1. The supervisor **had not been assigning**
2. The weather **had not been improving**
3. Jodi and I **had not been following**
4. They **had not been checking**
5. She **had not been ignoring**
6. You **had not been getting**
7. I **had not been exercising**

10-3

1. He **hadn't been expecting**
2. It'd **been changing**
3. We'd **been hoping**
4. They **hadn't been looking**
5. She'd **been lying**
6. You **hadn't been joking**
7. I'd **been thinking**

10-4

1. **Had** you **been working** too hard?
2. **Had** he **been living** by himself?
3. **Had** she **been talking** too loudly?
4. **Had** they **been waiting** a long time?
5. **Had** the suspect **been telling** the truth?

10-5

1. Who **had been making** the arrangements?
2. How long **had** he **been thinking** about moving?
3. What **had** they **been using** before the new shipment arrived?
4. Who **had been leading** the discussion when the argument started?
5. How long **had** they **been working** on the project?

Part III The Future Tense
Unit 11 Simple Future

11-1
1. will commute
2. will require
3. will give
4. will visit
5. will be
6. will announce
7. will leave
8. will complete
9. will call
10. will expand

11-2
1. They'll believe
2. I'll deliver
3. You'll like
4. It'll end
5. He'll help
6. She'll introduce
7. We'll sit

11-3
1. He **will not finish** by tomorrow.
2. You **will not have** a lot of fun there.
3. She **will not know** the answer.
4. We **will not ignore** the problem.
5. They **will not keep** your secret.
6. He **will not lie** to you.
7. I **will not need** help with my homework.
8. Marian **will not be** alone.
9. I **will not mention** your name.
10. They **will not be** late.

11-4
1. He **won't finish** by tomorrow.
2. You **won't have** a lot of fun there.
3. She **won't know** the answer.
4. We **won't ignore** the problem.
5. They **won't keep** your secret.
6. He **won't lie** to you.
7. I **won't need** help with my homework.
8. Marian **won't be** alone.
9. I **won't mention** your name.
10. They **won't be** late.

11-5
1. **Will** they **tell** us on Friday?
2. **Will** she **report** the incident?
3. **Will** you **laugh** at my mistakes?
4. **Will** Mitch **need** some help?
5. **Will** the noise **bother** you?
6. **Will** he **lend** us some money?
7. **Will** Dr. Silvis **be** free at 4:00?
8. **Will** we **meet** later?
9. **Will** they **use** your plan?
10. **Will** Federal Express **deliver** the package to our house?

11-6

1. Who **will repair** his car?
2. When **will** the class **meet**?
3. When **will** Rhonda **finish** the report?
4. How much **will** it **cost**?
5. Whom **will** they **blame** for the mistake?
6. Who **will choose** the scholarship winners?
7. How long **will** the supervisor **be** on vacation?
8. What **will** they **complain** about?
9. Who **will lead** the discussion?
10. When **will** the dance group **perform**?

Unit 12 *Be Going To*

12-1

1. is going to be
2. are going to build
3. is going to buy
4. am going to cancel
5. are going to climb
6. are going to celebrate
7. is going to call
8. is going to come
9. is going to deliver
10. are going to elect

12-2

1. is going to   imminent action
2. will   commitment
3. am going to   imminent action
4. is going to   imminent action
5. will   commitment

12-3

1. Taxes **are not going to increase**
2. It **is not going to snow**
3. We **are not going to go**
4. He **is not going to listen**
5. She **is not going to travel**
6. You **are not going to have**
7. I **am not going to forget**

12-4

1. **He's not going to come** OR **He isn't going to come**
2. **It's going to rain**
3. **I'm going to clean**
4. **They're not going to believe** OR **They aren't going to believe**
5. **She's not going to call** OR **She isn't going to call**
6. **You're going to do**
7. **I'm not going to cook**

12-5

1. **Are** they **going to consider** your proposal?
2. **Are** you **going to enter** the park at the north gate?
3. **Is** the doctor **going to explain** the procedure?
4. **Are** we **going to explore** our new neighborhood today?
5. **Is** he **going to fix** it for free?
6. **Are** you **going to follow** us?
7. **Is** she **going to get** into trouble?
8. **Is** it **going to happen** soon?
9. **Is** he **going to like** this idea?
10. **Are** we **going to look** for a new apartment today?

12-6

1. Who **is going to move** to Chile?
2. How much **is** she **going to earn**?
3. When **are** we **going to eat**?
4. When **are** they **going to improve** the roads?
5. When **are** you **going to develop** the film?
6. Whom **are** they **going to invite**?
7. When **are** the legislators **going to discuss** the bill?
8. Where **is** he **going to live**?
9. Who **is going to march** in the parade?
10. When **is** the eclipse **going to occur**?

Unit 13 Future Progressive (*Will Be* Verb + *-ing*)

13-1

1. will be representing
2. will be leaving
3. will be following
4. will be waiting
5. will be watching
6. will be producing
7. will be providing
8. will be snowing
9. will be wearing
10. will be opening

13-2

1. They **will not be appearing**
2. It **will not be starting**
3. We **will not be reading**
4. He **will not be arriving**
5. She **will not be staying**
6. You **will not be living**
7. I **will not be making**

13-3

1. He **won't be joining**
2. **It'll be affecting**
3. **I'll be treating**
4. They **won't be needing**
5. She **won't be arriving**
6. **you'll be flying**
7. I **won't be thinking**

13-4

1. **Will I be seeing** you next week?
2. **Will** they **be traveling** by bus?
3. **Will** Takamitsu **be assisting** Heather?
4. **Will** they **be offering** special packages at the end of the season?
5. **Will** you **be checking** your e-mail daily?

13-5

1. Who **will be taking** notes?
2. Who **will be receiving** an award?
3. Where **will** they **be sitting**?
4. How far **will** you **be driving** on your first day?
5. When **will** she **be finishing** her project?

Unit 14 Future Perfect

14-1
1. will have left
2. will have written
3. will have introduced
4. will have flown
5. will have eaten

14-2
1. You **will not have rested**
2. they **will not have eaten**
3. We **will not have finished**
4. Mark **will not have slept**
5. She **will not have saved**

14-3
1. **they'll have completed**
2. he **won't have finished**
3. **you'll have recovered**
4. They **won't have made**
5. **She'll have given**

14-4
1. **Will** the landscape **have changed** by the time he's an adult?
2. By July 11, **will** we **have made** our decision?
3. By the time you start your new job, **will** you **have finished** your degree?
4. By the time we get home, **will** he **have called** already?
5. When we get to the movie theater, **will** the movie **have started** already?

14-5
1. **will have become** the record holder?
2. **will** she **have lived** in Moscow when her family arrives?
3. **will** Andy **have run**?
4. **will** they **have spent**?
5. **will** he **have written**?

Unit 15 Future Perfect Progressive

15-1
1. will have been living
2. will have been discussing
3. will have been practicing
4. will have been playing
5. will have been working

15-2
1. they **will not have been talking**
2. the subways **will not have been running**
3. they **will not have been producing**
4. the dance troupe **will not have been performing**
5. she **will not have been working**

15-3
1. they **won't have been working**
2. **they'll have been broadcasting**
3. **we'll have been renting**
4. **they'll have been returning**
5. he **won't have been assisting**

15-4

1. **will have been making** the schedule for five years?
2. **will** the dance contestants **have been dancing**?
3. **will** we **have been using** this computer?
4. **will** you **have been working** on this paper?
5. **will** Ron **have been keeping** a journal?

Part IV Imperative, Passive, and Hypothetical Conditional
Unit 16 Imperative

16-1

1. answer
2. Have
3. Open
4. be
5. Finish
6. Call
7. Bake
8. Meet
9. Turn
10. Drive

16-2

1. Do not be
   Don't be late!
2. Do not run
   Don't run on the deck of the pool.
3. Do not forget
   Don't forget your homework.
4. Do not lie
   Don't lie to me.
5. Do not shout
   Don't shout at us.
6. Do not drink
   Don't drink the water.
7. Do not start
   Don't start the car yet.
8. Do not blame
   Don't blame me.
9. Do not boil
   Don't boil the water too long.
10. Do not break
    Don't break anything.

16-3

1. Let's make
2. Let's not forget
3. Let's not stay
4. Let's call
5. Let's celebrate

Unit 17 Passive

17-1

1. will be rewarded
   He'll be rewarded for his work.
2. were affected
   They **were affected** by the changes in the tax law.
3. are delivered
   They're delivered daily.

4. are grown
   They're grown in Idaho.
5. were announced
   They **were announced** yesterday.
6. will be changed
   They'll be changed next week.
7. will be rescheduled
   It'll be rescheduled.
8. are invited
   They're invited to the party.
9. was blamed
   She **was blamed** for the error.
10. was destroyed
    It **was destroyed**.

17-2

1. is being broadcast (OR broadcasted)
   It's being broadcast (OR **broadcasted**) around the world.
2. are being developed
   They're being developed.
3. was being carried
   It **was being carried** to the plane when one of the suitcases popped open.
4. were being discussed
   They **were being discussed** when we arrived.
5. is being considered
   It's being considered.
6. were being checked
   They **were being checked** when the alarm rang.
7. are being elected
   They're being elected this year.
8. is being closed
   It's being closed because of safety problems.
9. were being ignored
   They **were being ignored** by the politicians.
10. are being collected
    They're being collected for the poor.

17-3

1. has been promoted
   He's been promoted.
2. will have been assigned
   They'll have been assigned by the time we arrive.
3. had been delayed
   They'd been delayed at the airport, so they were late.
4. will have been finished
   It'll have been finished when the director meets with us.
5. had been praised
   It'd been praised highly.
6. will have been notified
   We'll have been notified of any problems before we leave.
7. have been made
   They've been made.
8. has been offered
   It's been offered to Laila.
9. has been revised
   It's been revised.
10. had been improved
    They'd been improved since my previous visit.

17-4

1. The game **was not canceled**.
2. Rita **has not been fired**.
3. By this time next year, the project **will not have been completed**.
4. Some of the important issues **are not being discussed**.
5. Our bags **are not being searched**.
6. Your x-rays **will not be returned** to you.
7. The recent findings **are not being presented** to the public.
8. The cell phone **had not been taken** from the car.
9. This computer **has not been used** before.
10. The document **is not being prepared** by the secretary.

17-5

1. **Were** all questions **answered**?
2. **Has** everyone **been notified** of the cancellation?
3. **Will** the basketball game **be broadcast** (OR **broadcasted**)?
4. **Is** the road being **repaired**?
5. **Had** enough evidence **been collected**?
6. **Was** he **impressed** by the report?
7. **Have** the costs for the project **been calculated**?
8. **Are** jobs **being cut**?
9. **Are** solutions to the problem **being explored**?
10. **Will** the clock **be fixed** tomorrow?

17-6

1. Who **has been elected**?
2. What **was explored**?
3. Who **was given** a scholarship?
4. What **is grown** in Hawaii?
5. Who **is being honored** at the special dinner tonight?
6. When **are** the invitations **being sent**?
7. When **were** the books **moved** to the new library?
8. Where **are** the new lights **being installed**?
9. How many credits **are required** for graduation?
10. What **was damaged** in the fire?

Unit 18 Hypothetical Conditional

18-1

1. were, would change
2. checked, would know
3. commuted, would cost
4. had, would go
5. visited, would meet
6. mailed, would receive
7. lowered, would shop
8. earned, would buy
9. exercised, would be
10. were, would tell

18-2

1. had rained, would have canceled
2. had been, would have been
3. had known, would have taken
4. had followed, would have been
5. had studied, would have passed
6. had been, would have received
7. had raised, would have protested
8. had repaired, would have left
9. had revised, would have been
10. had been, would have hired

Part V Phrasal Verbs and Modal Auxiliary Verbs
Unit 19 Phrasal Verbs

19-1
go/goes out, went out, will go out
am/is/are going out, was/were going out, will be going out
has/have gone out, had gone out, will have gone out
has/have been going out, had been going out, will have been going out

19-2
1. has taken away
2. was putting on
3. will find out
4. am looking up
5. will be signing up
6. had put off
7. will have read through
8. has been putting out
9. will have been going over
10. take out
11. pointed out
12. had been paying back

19-3
am/is/are set up, was/were set up, will be set up
am/is are being set up, was/were being set up
has/have been set up, had been set up, will have been set up

19-4
1. had been eaten up
2. was blocked in
3. has been put out
4. will be blown up
5. is being slowed down
6. is brought about
7. was being broken into
8. will have been brought out

19-5
1. She **brought** the books **back** yesterday.
   She **brought** them **back** yesterday.
2. They **called** the game **off**.
   They **called** it **off**.
3. I **checked** the book **out** on Monday.
   I **checked** it **out** on Monday.
4. I **crossed** some names **out**.
   I **crossed** them **out**.
5. Someone **turned** the washing machine **off**.
   Someone **turned** it **off**.
6. I **called** my parents **up** last night.
   I **called** them **up** last night.
7. She **closed** her suitcase **up** and put it on the scale.
   She **closed** it **up** and put it on the scale.
8. I **cleaned** my desk **out** this morning.
   I **cleaned** it **out** this morning.
9. She **wrote** the number **down**.
   She **wrote** it **down**.
10. They **gave** their old furniture **away**.
    They **gave** it **away**.
11. Victor **helped** his sister **out**.
    Victor **helped** her **out**.
12. She **took** a map **down** and gave it to us.
    She **took** it **down** and gave it to us.

19-6

1. Jacob **is not writing down** the address.
2. She **has not booted up** the computer.
3. The hot weather **was not wearing** us **down**.
4. The books **were not brought back** yesterday.
5. The painting on the sidewalk **has not been washed off**.
6. I **am not bringing** my friend over tonight.
7. They **do not vote down** most proposals.
8. He **did not make up** the story.
9. I **will not print out** my paper on that printer.
10. The report **was not turned in** on time.
11. She **did not set it down** carefully.
12. They **had not been locked out** of their car before.

Unit 20 Modal Auxiliary Verbs

20-1

1. will
2. should
3. may
4. must
5. can
6. would
7. May
8. must
9. may
10. will
11. should
12. Can
13. may
14. would

20-2

1. are going to
2. ought to
3. used to
4. have to
5. is able to
6. used to
7. ought to
8. have to
9. are able to
10. is going to

20-3

1. was going to
2. ought to
3. had to
4. was able to
5. was going to
6. ought to
7. had to
8. were able to

20-4

1. might [modal], be able to [semi-modal]
2. are going to [semi-modal], be able to [semi-modal]
3. might [modal], have to [semi-modal]
4. are going to [semi-modal], have to [semi-modal]
5. will [modal], have to [semi-modal]

20-5
1. You **should not**
2. We **cannot**
3. Martin **is not able to**
4. The supervisor **is not going to**
5. They **may not**
6. You **must not**
7. we **would not**
8. they **will not**
9. I **do not have to**
10. You **should not**

20-6
1. You **shouldn't smoke** in this restaurant.
2. We **can't escape** the heat today.
3. Martin **isn't able to find** his books.
4. The supervisor **isn't going to be** happy.
5. No contraction possible
6. You **mustn't tell** anyone.
7. When we were little, we **wouldn't go** inside until 10:00.
8. For some reason, they **won't answer** their phone.
9. Tomorrow, I **don't have to get up** early.
10. You **shouldn't worry** so much.

20-7
1. should have
2. should have
3. should have OR could have OR ought to have
4. may have been OR might have been
5. must have
6. should have
7. may have OR might have
8. should have
9. must have
10. should have been OR could have been OR ought to have been

Part VI Gerund and Infinitive Complements
Unit 21 Gerunds

21-1
1. having
2. being surprised
3. having mentioned
4. trying
5. having been invited
6. eating
7. having been chosen
8. reviewing
9. having been
10. being treated
11. stopping
12. being given
13. playing
14. damaging
15. being introduced

21-2
The verbs and possible gerunds are provided. Other parts of the sentence may vary.
1. I **enjoy visiting** my relatives.
2. I **have avoided writing** letters.
3. I **dislike doing** chores on the weekend.

4. I **liked being told** the story about the three little pigs.
5. I **miss seeing** my friend Judy.

Unit 22 Infinitives

22-1

1. to be working
2. to pay
3. to have earned
4. to have fainted
5. to be hired
6. to help
7. to have been leaked
8. to be networking
9. to have received
10. to be given
11. to meet
12. to stay
13. to turn in
14. to move
15. to close

22-2

The verbs and infinitives are provided. Other parts of the sentence may vary.
1. I **plan to go** to the park.
2. I **intend to be** right here.
3. I **need to buy** a new notebook.
4. I **want to have** a pizza.
5. I **expect to study** chemistry.

22-3

1. him to exercise
2. us to attend
3. my sister to ride
4. me to turn
5. people to touch
6. Brent and me to be
7. local artists to hang
8. the protesters to leave
9. me to rethink
10. employers to provide
11. Robyn to major
12. everyone to conserve

Unit 23 Gerunds or Infinitives

23-1

1. infinitive: to rain	no significant change in meaning
2. infinitive: to bring	memory to perform action
3. gerund: quitting	memory of action
4. infinitive: to talk	no significant change in meaning
5. gerund: going	vivid depiction
6. infinitive: to clean up	hypothetical occurrence
7. gerund: returning	memory of action
8. gerund: throwing	vivid depiction
9. infinitive: to make	no significant change in meaning
10. infinitive: to take	potential occurrence